GW00771162

Tony bellew

Tony bellew

Tony bellew

All rights reserved. No part of this publication may be reproduced, distributed, or transmitted in any form or by any means, including photocopying, recording, or other electronic or mechanical methods, without the prior written permission of the publisher, except in the case of brief quotations embodied in critical reviews and certain other noncommercial uses permitted by copyright law. Copyright ©

Karen Lee, 2023.

Tony bellew

Tablet of content

INTRODUCTION

1.1 Early life

1.2 Background

CHAPTER 2: THE FIGHTER MIND

CHAPTER 3: PERSONAL LIFE

CHAPTER 4: TONY BELLEW

CHAPTER 5: Retirement Transition

CHAPTER 9: Entry Into Boxing

CHAPTER 29: Life Lessons and Legacy

CHAPTER 24: Instant Analysis

CHAPTER 33: Early Indications of Punching Power

CHAPTER 34: The Art of Boxing

CHAPTER 30: The Final Bell

CHAPTER 19: Tony Bellew: A Puncher's Path

CHAPTER 20: Heartfelt Battles

Tony bellew

Tony bellew

INTRODUCTION

In "Tony Bellew: The Art of Boxing Brilliance," we step into the electrifying world of one of boxing's most captivating figures. From the gritty streets to the grandeur of championship bouts, this book explores the dynamic career and indomitable spirit of Tony Bellew, a man who transcended the sport to become a true maestro of the sweet science.

As we navigate the pages of this narrative, we delve into Bellew's early life, a journey that laid the foundation for his ascent into the world of boxing. From the raw determination of his amateur days to the polished precision of his professional career, we witness the evolution of a pugilist whose artistry extends beyond the ring ropes.

Tony bellew

Within these chapters, the reader is invited to witness Bellew's rise through the ranks, his battles against formidable opponents, and the triumphs that solidified his place in boxing history. Yet, "The Art of Boxing Brilliance" is more than a chronicle of victories and defeats; it unravels the intricate layers of Bellew's fighting style, his mental fortitude, and the strategic brilliance that defined his approach to the sport.

Beyond the squared circle, this book explores Bellew's life outside of boxing—the personal struggles, triumphs, and the indelible mark he left on the sport's landscape. As we embark on this journey, we gain insights into the artistry that is Tony Bellew, a fighter whose legacy is etched not only in championships but in the hearts of those who witnessed his unparalleled skill and unwavering determination. Join us as we unravel "The Art of Boxing Brilliance" and discover the essence of a true boxing virtuoso.

CHAPTER 1: WHO IS TONY BELLEW

As of my last knowledge update in January 2022, Tony Bellew is a retired British professional boxer and actor. Born on November 30, 1982, in Liverpool, England, Bellew had a successful career in boxing, primarily competing in the cruiserweight and heavyweight divisions.

Bellew gained widespread recognition for his performances in the ring and his charismatic personality outside of it. He became the WBC cruiserweight champion after defeating Ilunga Makabu in 2016. Bellew also engaged in notable fights against high-profile opponents, including his clashes with David Haye.

In addition to his boxing career, Tony Bellew ventured into acting, making appearances in films such as "Creed" and "Creed II," adding another dimension to his public profile.

It's important to note that my information might be outdated, and there may have been developments in Tony Bellew's life or career since then.

1.1 Early life

Born on November 30, 1982, in Liverpool, England, Anthony "Tony" Bellew's early life was shaped by the gritty streets of the city. Growing up in a working-class environment, Bellew discovered his passion for boxing at an early age. The tough surroundings fueled his determination, and he soon found an outlet for his energy and ambition in the local boxing gyms.

Bellew's journey into the sport began as an amateur, where he honed his skills and developed a reputation for

Tony bellew

his raw talent and tenacity. His early experiences in the ring laid the foundation for what would become a remarkable career.

Beyond the boxing gloves, Bellew navigated the challenges of his upbringing, forging a path that would lead him to become a prominent figure in British and international boxing. The resilience and drive he exhibited during his formative years would later define his character as a professional boxer.

These early life experiences not only shaped Tony Bellew as a fighter but also contributed to the unwavering determination and authenticity that would make him a beloved figure in the world of boxing. The streets of Liverpool provided the backdrop for the early chapters of his life, setting the stage for the compelling journey that would unfold in the years to come.

1.2 Background

It appears you're asking for more information, but I'd appreciate clarification on what specific background you're interested in. Are you looking for Tony Bellew's overall background, including his career, personal life, or any specific aspect? Please provide more details so I can offer a more targeted response.

CHAPTER 2: THE FIGHTER MIND

Tony Bellew's approach to boxing goes beyond physical prowess; it delves into the intricate realm of "The Fighter's Mind." In the ring, Bellew showcased not only technical skill but also mental fortitude, a strategic mindset, and an unyielding determination that set him apart.

Tony Bellew's mental toughness was a defining aspect of his boxing career, elevating him to triumphs and helping him navigate challenges with resilience. Here are key facets of his mental toughness:

1. **Adversity as Motivation:** Bellew transformed adversity into motivation, using setbacks as fuel for improvement. His ability to bounce back from defeats showcased a mental resilience that set the stage for later successes.

Tony bellew

2. **Focus Under Pressure:** In the heat of competition, Bellew maintained a focused mindset. Whether facing formidable opponents or enduring the pressure of high-stakes bouts, his mental toughness shone through, allowing him to perform under demanding circumstances.

3. **Embracing Challenges:** Rather than shying away from challenges, Bellew embraced them. His mental toughness was evident in his willingness to take on tough opponents and step into weight classes that presented new challenges, demonstrating a fearless mentality.

4. **Composure in the Ring:** Maintaining composure in the midst of a boxing match is a testament to mental toughness. Bellew's ability to stay composed, make strategic decisions, and execute his game plan showcased a mental fortitude that contributed to his success.

5. **Resilience After Setbacks:** Throughout his career, Bellew faced setbacks and defeats. However, his mental toughness became apparent in how he rebounded from these setbacks, learning from each experience and returning stronger in subsequent fights.

6. **Positive Mindset:** Bellew often exhibited a positive mindset, both in and out of the ring. This optimistic approach contributed to his mental resilience, allowing him to stay focused on goals and maintain determination even in challenging situations.

7. **Adaptability:** The ability to adapt to evolving circumstances is a mark of mental toughness. Bellew displayed adaptability in adjusting his strategies during fights, showcasing a versatile and resilient mindset.

In the realm of professional boxing, mental toughness is often as critical as physical prowess. Tony Bellew's career serves as a testament to the power of a strong and resilient mindset, demonstrating that success in the sport goes beyond the physicality of punches and training.

Tony bellew

2.1 Mental Toughness:** Explore the mental resilience that propelled Bellew through challenges inside and outside the ring. Learn how he turned adversity into motivation, emerging stronger with each setback.

2. **Strategic Brilliance:** Enter the strategic mind of a fighter who tactically approached each opponent. From studying weaknesses to adapting mid-bout, Bellew's cerebral approach to boxing is dissected, revealing the artistry behind his victories.

3.1Focus and Discipline:** Uncover the disciplined mindset that guided Bellew's training and preparation. Delve into the rituals and mental conditioning that contributed to his consistent performances on fight night.

Tony Bellew's focus and discipline were integral to his success as a professional boxer. These attributes permeated every aspect of his career, contributing to his achievements in the ring and beyond:

Tony bellew

1. **Training Dedication:** Bellew's training routine was characterized by unwavering dedication. He approached each session with focus, committing to the physical and mental demands of preparing for high-stakes bouts.

2. **Strategic Preparation:** His focus extended beyond physical conditioning to strategic preparation. Bellew meticulously studied his opponents, developing game plans that capitalized on their weaknesses and showcased his strengths.

3. **Weight Management:** Competing in different weight classes requires strict discipline in weight management. Bellew's ability to maintain the necessary discipline in his diet and training allowed him to compete effectively across various divisions.

4. **Consistency in Performance:** Bellew's career was marked by consistent performances. His focus on maintaining a high standard of excellence ensured that he approached every fight with the same level of

commitment, regardless of the opponent or the significance of the bout.

5. **Mental Toughness:** Focus and discipline played a pivotal role in Bellew's mental toughness. Whether facing adversity or navigating the pressure of significant matches, he exhibited mental resilience grounded in his disciplined mindset.

6. **Professionalism:** Bellew conducted himself with professionalism both inside and outside the ring. His disciplined approach to the promotional aspects of the sport, media obligations, and public appearances reflected a commitment to the overall professionalism of boxing.

7. **Goal-Oriented Approach:** Bellew's focus on specific goals guided his career. Whether aiming for a championship title or seeking to overcome a particular opponent, his disciplined approach kept him on a path of continuous improvement.

Tony bellew

In examining Tony Bellew's focus and discipline, it becomes clear that these qualities were not just tools for success but integral components of his character. They underpinned his training, strategic approach, and overall mindset, contributing significantly to his accomplishments in the demanding world of professional boxing.

4. **Emotional Intelligence:** Beyond physicality, Bellew's success hinged on understanding the emotional dynamics of the sport. Explore how he navigated the mental chess game, deciphering opponents and seizing pivotal moments.

5. **Motivational Reservoir:** Discover the wellsprings of motivation that fueled Bellew's journey. Whether it was family, personal goals, or a desire to leave a lasting legacy, his inner drive becomes a focal point in understanding "The Fighter's Mind."

In "Tony Bellew: The Fighter's Mind," readers are invited to unravel the psychological layers that shaped a

Tony bellew

boxer's journey. From the intense focus before a fight to the reflective moments of a champion, this exploration goes beyond the physicality of the sport, offering a glimpse into the mental landscape of a true warrior.

CHAPTER 3: PERSONAL LIFE

Tony Bellew's personal life adds depth to the narrative of the accomplished boxer, providing insight into the man beyond the ring:

1. **Family Ties:** Bellew's personal life is characterized by strong family bonds. A proud father and husband, he often spoke about the importance of his family as a source of motivation and support throughout his career.

2. **Liverpool Roots:** Raised in Liverpool, England, Bellew's personal identity is closely tied to his working-class roots. The city's culture and spirit played a role in shaping his character and approach to both life and boxing.

3. **Early Influences:** Growing up in Liverpool's vibrant but challenging environment, Bellew's personal journey was influenced by early experiences that fueled his drive to succeed. These experiences, both positive and challenging, contributed to the fighter and man he would become.

4.1Outside Interests:** Beyond boxing, Bellew displayed diverse interests. His involvement in acting, with roles in films like "Creed" and "Creed II," showcased a passion for exploring different facets of the entertainment industry.

Beyond his illustrious boxing career, Tony Bellew has demonstrated a range of outside interests that showcase his diverse talents and passions:

1. **Acting Career:** One of the most notable aspects of Bellew's outside interests is his foray into acting. He took on acting roles in major films, including "Creed" and its sequel "Creed II." His performances in these

films showcased his ability to transition seamlessly from the boxing ring to the big screen.

2. **Media Commentary:** Bellew extended his influence beyond the realm of participation, becoming a sought-after media personality. He provided insightful commentary on boxing matches and related events, sharing his expertise with audiences and contributing to the sport's narrative.

3. **Public Speaking:** With his charismatic personality and articulate communication style, Bellew has engaged in public speaking engagements. Whether sharing insights from his boxing career or discussing broader topics, his public speaking contributions have added depth to his post-boxing pursuits.

4. **Promotional Activities:** As a professional athlete, Bellew engaged in various promotional activities associated with boxing events. His involvement in promoting fights and events showcased not only his

commitment to the sport but also his understanding of its promotional aspects.

5. **Fitness and Training:** Bellew has maintained a connection to the world of fitness and training even after retirement. Sharing workout routines, training tips, and insights into his fitness regimen, he continues to inspire others to adopt a healthy and active lifestyle.

6. **Social Media Presence:** Bellew is active on social media platforms, providing fans with glimpses into his daily life, perspectives on current events, and updates on his various interests. His social media presence allows him to connect with a broader audience beyond the traditional realms of sports.

These outside interests collectively illustrate Tony Bellew's multifaceted personality and his ability to seamlessly transition into different roles beyond the boxing arena. Whether on the screen, behind the microphone, or in the public eye, Bellew continues to make meaningful contributions that extend beyond the boundaries of his initial sporting career.

5. **Community Engagement:** Bellew maintained a connection with his community, and his personal life included various engagements with local initiatives and charities. His commitment to giving back reflects a sense of responsibility to the community that shaped him.

6. **Balancing Act:** Navigating the demands of a professional boxing career and personal life requires balance. Bellew's ability to strike this balance, juggling the intensity of training and competition with family commitments, adds a human dimension to his story.

7. **Retirement Transition:** The transition from an active boxing career to retirement often marks a significant chapter in a boxer's personal life. Bellew's post-retirement activities and pursuits provide a glimpse into his evolving identity beyond the world of sports.

Tony bellew

Understanding Tony Bellew's personal life provides a more comprehensive picture of the man behind the gloves. It unveils the values, relationships, and experiences that shaped him, offering a narrative that extends beyond the boundaries of the boxing ring.

CHAPTER 4: TONY BELLEW

Tony Bellew's venture into acting adds a compelling dimension to his multifaceted career. Here's a closer look at his role as "Tony Bellew: The Actor":

1.1 Film Debut:** Bellew made a notable entry into the world of acting with his debut in the film "Creed" (2015). His performance in this critically acclaimed movie marked the beginning of his acting journey.

1

Tony Bellew made a notable entry into the world of acting with his film debut in "Creed" (2015). This marked a significant transition from the boxing ring to the silver screen, showcasing Bellew's versatility beyond the realm of sports.

In "Creed," Bellew took on the role of "Pretty" Ricky Conlan, a fictional world champion boxer with a charismatic yet formidable persona. The film, which is a spin-off and sequel to the iconic "Rocky" series, not only provided Bellew with a platform to showcase his acting skills but also allowed him to bring an authentic boxing background to the character.

Bellew's portrayal of "Pretty" Ricky Conlan was praised for its authenticity and depth. His experience as a professional boxer translated into a convincing on-screen presence, earning recognition from both fans and critics. The film's success and positive reception further solidified Bellew's position as a crossover talent in the entertainment industry.

This film debut marked the beginning of Tony Bellew's acting journey, setting the stage for subsequent roles and projects that would explore his capabilities as an actor beyond his accomplished career in professional boxing.

2. **"Pretty" Ricky Conlan:** In "Creed," Bellew portrayed the character "Pretty" Ricky Conlan, a fictional world champion boxer. His authentic background in boxing brought credibility to the role,

earning praise for his on-screen presence and authenticity.

3. **Sequel Success:** Following the success of "Creed," Bellew reprised his role in the sequel, "Creed II" (2018). His involvement in both films showcased not only his acting skills but also his ability to seamlessly transition from the real-world boxing ring to the scripted drama of Hollywood.

4. **Character Range:** Bellew's foray into acting allowed him to explore different facets of character portrayal. While "Pretty" Ricky Conlan showcased his familiarity with the boxing world, it also demonstrated his ability to inhabit complex characters on screen.

5. **Diverse Projects:** Beyond the "Creed" series, Bellew's acting career hinted at a potential for diverse projects. Whether through dramatic roles, action sequences, or character-driven narratives, his involvement in film hinted at a willingness to explore a range of roles.

Tony bellew

6. **Collaboration with Industry Professionals:**
Working alongside acclaimed actors and filmmakers in
the entertainment industry, Bellew's acting pursuits
reflected a collaborative spirit and a desire to learn from
and contribute to the broader world of film.

Tony Bellew's acting career added a new chapter to his
story, showcasing his versatility and expanding his
influence beyond the boxing ring. It demonstrated that
his talents and presence could captivate audiences not
only in the sporting arena but also on the silver screen.

CHAPTER 5: Retirement Transition

Tony Bellew's transition from an active boxing career to retirement marked a significant chapter in his life. This period was characterized by various aspects, illustrating his adaptability and the evolution of his identity beyond the boxing ring:

1. **Reflection and Legacy:** Upon retirement, Bellew took time to reflect on his accomplishments and the impact he had made in the world of boxing. This introspective period allowed him to assess his legacy and the mark he had left on the sport.

2. **Post-Retirement Pursuits:** Beyond the ring, Bellew explored new avenues and pursuits. His involvement in acting continued, demonstrating a seamless transition from a career in professional sports to the entertainment industry.

3. Media Roles:** Bellew leveraged his expertise and charisma as a boxing commentator and analyst. His insights into the sport, combined with his articulate communication style, made him a sought-after figure in the media landscape, further solidifying his presence in the boxing community.

Tony Bellew seamlessly transitioned into various media roles following his retirement from professional boxing, utilizing his charisma and insights to become a notable figure in the media landscape:

1. **Boxing Commentator:** Bellew brought his in-depth knowledge of boxing and his firsthand experience in the ring to the commentary booth. Serving as a boxing commentator, he provided expert analysis during live broadcasts of matches, enhancing the viewing experience for audiences.

2. **Analyst on Boxing Shows:** Beyond live commentary, Bellew appeared as an analyst on

boxing-related shows. His articulate communication style and ability to break down fights made him a sought-after figure for pre-match analysis and post-fight breakdowns.

3. **Television Appearances:** Bellew expanded his media presence through appearances on television programs. These appearances ranged from sports talk shows to broader entertainment platforms, allowing him to connect with diverse audiences and showcase his personality beyond the boxing realm.

4. **Radio Contributions:** Bellew extended his reach to the airwaves, contributing to radio discussions on boxing and related topics. His engaging presence and articulate commentary translated well to the radio format, further solidifying his position as a media personality.

5. **Podcast Guest and Host:** Bellew embraced the world of podcasts, both as a guest on various shows and as a host. Participating in discussions and sharing his

experiences, he utilized the podcast platform to connect with fans and provide unique insights into the world of boxing.

6. **Social Media Presence:** Active on social media platforms, Bellew engaged with fans and shared updates on his media endeavors. His social media presence became a valuable extension of his media roles, allowing for direct interaction with a global audience.

7. **Interviews and Media Appearances:** Bellew's retirement brought increased demand for interviews and media appearances. Whether discussing his own career, commenting on current events in boxing, or sharing personal insights, he became a respected voice in the media landscape.

Tony Bellew's media roles showcase not only his expertise in boxing but also his ability to connect with audiences across different platforms. His transition from athlete to media personality demonstrates a versatility that goes beyond the physicality of the sport, solidifying his presence as a respected and engaging figure in the world of sports media.

4. **Fitness and Well-being:** The transition to retirement often involves a shift in focus from intense training to overall fitness and well-being. Bellew maintained a commitment to fitness, sharing aspects of his post-boxing training routines and encouraging others to adopt a healthy lifestyle.

5. **Public Speaking Engagements:** Bellew engaged in public speaking, sharing his experiences, insights, and motivational messages. His transition to public speaking showcased his ability to inspire others with the lessons learned from his boxing journey.

6. **Community Engagement:** Retired from professional competition, Bellew remained connected to his community. Whether through charity events, community initiatives, or philanthropy, he continued to

contribute to causes beyond the scope of his athletic career.

7. **Advisory and Mentorship Roles:** Bellew, drawing on his extensive experience in the boxing world, took on advisory and mentorship roles. His guidance and support for emerging talents reflected a commitment to passing on knowledge and contributing to the future of the sport.

Tony Bellew's retirement transition demonstrates not only his adaptability but also his proactive approach to shaping the narrative of his post-boxing life. The chapters beyond retirement reveal a man who continues to evolve, embracing new challenges, and leaving an enduring impact on multiple facets of the sports and entertainment landscape.

Tony bellew

CHAPTER 6:Personal Insights on Career and Life

Tony Bellew, known for his candid and straightforward demeanor, has shared several personal insights on his career and life, offering a glimpse into his mindset and values:

1. **Passion for Boxing:** Bellew often emphasized his genuine love for the sport of boxing. His passion for the sweet science was a driving force throughout his career, evident in both his performances in the ring and his discussions about the sport.

2. **Resilience in the Face of Challenges:** Reflecting on his career, Bellew spoke openly about facing challenges and setbacks. His resilience in overcoming obstacles, both inside and outside the ring, became a defining feature of his narrative.

3. **Balancing Family and Career:** Family played a central role in Bellew's life, and he frequently spoke about the balancing act between his career as a

professional boxer and his responsibilities as a husband and father. This theme added a personal touch to his public persona.

4. **Transition to Acting:** Discussing his transition to acting, Bellew shared insights into the challenges and rewards of navigating a new industry. His willingness to embrace different opportunities highlighted a sense of adaptability and a desire for continuous growth.

5. **Appreciation for the Fans:** Bellew expressed deep gratitude for the support of his fans throughout his boxing career. He acknowledged the impact of fan support on his motivation and success, fostering a strong connection with the boxing community.

6. **Reflecting on Achievements:** As his career progressed, Bellew took moments to reflect on his achievements. Whether winning titles or participating in iconic bouts, he shared reflections on the significance of these milestones in shaping his legacy.

7. **Embracing Challenges:** Bellew's career was marked by a willingness to take on challenges, often facing opponents in higher weight classes. His approach reflected a fearless mentality and a belief in his own abilities to overcome challenges.

8. **Pride in Liverpool Roots:** Proud of his Liverpool roots, Bellew often spoke about the influence of his hometown on his identity. The city's spirit and culture became integral to his personal and professional narrative.

These personal insights offer a more nuanced understanding of Tony Bellew as not just a boxer but as an individual navigating the complexities of a dynamic career and a rich personal life. His openness in sharing these perspectives contributed to the authenticity that defined his public image.

CHAPTER 7: Strategic Preparation

Tony Bellew's strategic preparation in boxing was a key element of his success, showcasing a meticulous approach to studying opponents and crafting effective game plans. Here are facets of his strategic preparation:

1. **Opponent Analysis:** Bellew dedicated significant time to studying his opponents. Analyzing their strengths, weaknesses, and fighting styles allowed him to tailor his strategy to exploit vulnerabilities and capitalize on opportunities.

2. **Adaptability:** One of Bellew's strengths was his ability to adapt mid-fight. His strategic preparation included scenarios for different situations, allowing him to make effective adjustments during bouts and respond intelligently to his opponent's tactics.

3. **Weight Class Considerations:** Competing in multiple weight classes, Bellew strategically selected opponents and made weight considerations based on the advantages he could leverage in each division. This approach showcased his strategic thinking beyond individual fights.

4. **Training Specifics:** His training camps were designed with the specific strengths and weaknesses of upcoming opponents in mind. This targeted training approach ensured that Bellew was physically and mentally prepared for the challenges posed by different adversaries.

5. **Ring IQ:** Bellew's strategic preparation extended to the development of a high boxing intelligence (Ring IQ). This encompassed a deep understanding of the sport, a keen awareness of the unfolding dynamics in the ring, and the ability to make split-second decisions to gain an edge.

6. **Game Plans for Specific Fights:** Each fight had its unique dynamics, and Bellew approached them with tailored game plans. Whether facing a power puncher or a tactician, he strategically planned his approach to maximize his chances of success.

7. **Psychological Warfare:** Bellew understood the psychological aspect of boxing. His strategic preparation involved not only physical readiness but also tactics to disrupt opponents' mental composure, creating advantages in the psychological warfare of the sport.

8. **Team Collaboration:** Working closely with his coaching team, Bellew's strategic preparation involved collaborative efforts. Coaches provided insights, analyzed opponents' styles, and contributed to the formulation of effective game plans.

9. **Conditioning:** Recognizing the importance of stamina in executing strategic plans, Bellew prioritized conditioning. His training camps included elements

focused on endurance, ensuring that he could maintain his strategic approach throughout the duration of a fight.

Conditioning was a cornerstone of Tony Bellew's training regimen, playing a crucial role in his success as a professional boxer. Here are key aspects of Bellew's conditioning:

1. **Endurance Training:** Bellew engaged in rigorous endurance training to ensure he could sustain a high level of activity throughout a bout. Long-distance running, cycling, and other cardiovascular exercises were integral to building and maintaining his endurance.

2. **High-Intensity Workouts:** Interval training and high-intensity workouts were incorporated to simulate the intense pace of boxing matches. These sessions focused on short bursts of maximum effort followed by periods of active recovery, enhancing both aerobic and anaerobic conditioning.

3. **Sparring Sessions:** Live sparring sessions were a vital component of Bellew's conditioning. These sessions not only honed his technical skills but also simulated the physical and mental demands of actual fights, contributing to his overall fitness.

4. **Sport-Specific Drills:** Conditioning drills specific to boxing movements were integrated into his training routine. Shadowboxing, bag work, and footwork exercises tailored to the demands of the ring were crucial for refining his skills while enhancing his cardiovascular fitness.

5. **Weight Management:** Given Bellew's movement across different weight classes, managing weight was a key aspect of his conditioning. This involved a balance between maintaining strength and endurance while making weight safely for each division.

6. **Functional Strength Training:** Bellew incorporated functional strength training to enhance his overall physical capabilities. This included exercises that

mimicked the movements and demands of boxing, contributing to his strength and conditioning specific to the sport.

7. **Mental Toughness Conditioning:** Conditioning wasn't solely physical for Bellew. Mental toughness was cultivated through challenging training scenarios, creating a mindset that could withstand the pressures and fatigue of championship-level fights.

8. **Recovery Protocols:** Adequate recovery was part of Bellew's conditioning strategy. This involved a combination of rest days, proper nutrition, and recovery techniques such as ice baths and massages to optimize recovery between intense training sessions.

9. **Adaptability:** Bellew's conditioning routine was adaptable, recognizing the need for adjustments based on the specific requirements of upcoming fights and opponents. This flexibility allowed him to tailor his training to the unique challenges of each bout.

Tony bellew

Tony Bellew's commitment to conditioning was evident in his ability to maintain a high level of performance throughout his career. His well-rounded approach, incorporating both physical and mental conditioning, contributed to his success in the ring and solidified his reputation as a formidable athlete.

Tony Bellew's strategic preparation was a holistic and dynamic process, showcasing his commitment to mastering the technical and mental aspects of boxing. This approach contributed significantly to his success in the ring and solidified his reputation as a strategic and tactically astute boxer.

CHAPTER 8: Media Roles

Tony Bellew seamlessly transitioned into various media roles following his retirement from professional boxing, utilizing his charisma and insights to become a notable figure in the media landscape:

1. **Boxing Commentator:** Bellew brought his in-depth knowledge of boxing and his firsthand experience in the ring to the commentary booth. Serving as a boxing commentator, he provided expert analysis during live broadcasts of matches, enhancing the viewing experience for audiences.

2. **Analyst on Boxing Shows:** Beyond live commentary, Bellew appeared as an analyst on boxing-related shows. His articulate communication style and ability to break down fights made him a

sought-after figure for pre-match analysis and post-fight breakdowns.

3. **Television Appearances:** Bellew expanded his media presence through appearances on television programs. These appearances ranged from sports talk shows to broader entertainment platforms, allowing him to connect with diverse audiences and showcase his personality beyond the boxing realm.

4. **Radio Contributions:** Bellew extended his reach to the airwaves, contributing to radio discussions on boxing and related topics. His engaging presence and articulate commentary translated well to the radio format, further solidifying his position as a media personality.

5. **Podcast Guest and Host:** Bellew embraced the world of podcasts, both as a guest on various shows and as a host. Participating in discussions and sharing his experiences, he utilized the podcast platform to connect

with fans and provide unique insights into the world of boxing.

6. **Social Media Presence:** Active on social media platforms, Bellew engaged with fans and shared updates on his media endeavors. His social media presence became a valuable extension of his media roles, allowing for direct interaction with a global audience.

7. **Interviews and Media Appearances:** Bellew's retirement brought increased demand for interviews and media appearances. Whether discussing his own career, commenting on current events in boxing, or sharing personal insights, he became a respected voice in the media landscape.

Tony Bellew's media roles showcase not only his expertise in boxing but also his ability to connect with audiences across different platforms. His transition from athlete to media personality demonstrates a versatility that goes beyond the physicality of the sport, solidifying

Tony bellew

his presence as a respected and engaging figure in the
world of sports media.

CHAPTER 9: Entry into Boxing

Tony Bellew's entry into boxing traces back to his early life and a journey that led him to pursue a career in the sweet science:

1. **Amateur Beginnings:** Bellew's foray into boxing began in his hometown of Liverpool, England, where he engaged in amateur boxing during his youth. The amateur circuit served as the initial training ground for honing his skills and developing a passion for the sport.

2. **Local Gym:** Like many aspiring boxers, Bellew found himself drawn to a local boxing gym. This marked the starting point of his formal training, where he would learn the fundamentals of the sport and lay the groundwork for his future as a professional fighter.

. **Amateur Achievements:** During his amateur career, Bellew achieved notable success. His performances in regional and national competitions not only showcased his talent but also garnered attention within the boxing community, setting the stage for a transition to the professional ranks.

4. **Decision to Go Pro:** Motivated by his love for boxing and the desire to compete at the highest level, Bellew made the decision to turn professional. This pivotal choice marked the beginning of a new chapter, where he would navigate the challenges and opportunities of the professional boxing world.

5. **Early Professional Career:** Bellew's early professional career was marked by a series of victories as he climbed the ranks in the cruiserweight division. His technical skills, power, and determination quickly distinguished him as a rising prospect in British boxing.

6. **Championship Aspirations:** As Bellew continued to build momentum in the professional ranks, his aspirations shifted towards championship glory. The

pursuit of titles and recognition on the world stage became a driving force in his career trajectory.

7. **Versatility in Weight Classes:** One notable aspect of Bellew's career is his versatility in moving across different weight classes. This adaptability allowed him to face a diverse range of opponents, showcasing his skills in various divisions.

8. **Iconic Bouts:** Bellew's journey included memorable and iconic bouts, each contributing to the narrative of his career. Notable matchups against respected opponents further solidified his status as a top-tier fighter.

Tony Bellew's entry into boxing represents a classic tale of a young enthusiast discovering his passion, dedicating himself to the sport, and ultimately making a significant impact in the professional ranks. His journey is not only marked by achievements in the ring but also by the resilience and determination that defined his pursuit of greatness in boxing.

CHAPTER 9: Iconic Bouts

Tony Bellew's career featured several iconic bouts that left a lasting impact on the boxing world, showcasing his skill, determination, and ability to perform under pressure. Here are some of the notable and iconic bouts in Tony Bellew's career:

1. **Tony Bellew vs. Ovill McKenzie I (2011):** In their first encounter, Bellew faced Ovill McKenzie for the Commonwealth light-heavyweight title. The bout, which ended in a controversial majority decision in favor of Bellew, set the stage for their later rematch.

2. **Tony Bellew vs. Edison Miranda (2012):** Bellew faced the experienced Edison Miranda in a crucial bout. Bellew showcased his skills, securing a ninth-round stoppage and solidifying his reputation as a rising star in the cruiserweight division.

3. **Tony Bellew vs. Nathan Cleverly II (2014):** This rematch was a highly anticipated showdown for the WBA (Regular) light-heavyweight title. Bellew sought redemption after a previous close loss to Cleverly. The fight went the distance, and Bellew emerged victorious via split decision, gaining a world title in the process.

4. **Tony Bellew vs. Ilunga Makabu (2016):** In a dramatic contest for the vacant WBC cruiserweight title, Bellew faced Ilunga Makabu. Bellew secured a stunning knockout victory in the third round, realizing his dream of becoming a world champion in front of his home crowd at Goodison Park.

5. **Tony Bellew vs. David Haye I (2017):** Moving up to heavyweight, Bellew took on former world champion David Haye in a highly publicized bout. Despite being the underdog, Bellew weathered an early storm and secured a surprising 11th-round stoppage, solidifying his status as a force in the heavyweight division.

6. **Tony Bellew vs. David Haye II (2018):** The rematch between Bellew and Haye had added drama, and Bellew once again emerged victorious, securing a fifth-round knockout. These back-to-back wins over Haye further elevated Bellew's profile in the heavyweight ranks.

7. **Tony Bellew vs. Oleksandr Usyk (2018):** In what would be his final professional bout, Bellew faced the undefeated Oleksandr Usyk for the undisputed cruiserweight title. Despite a spirited effort, Bellew succumbed to a knockout in the eighth round. The bout showcased Bellew's courage and competitiveness against one of the best in the division.

Each of these bouts contributed to the narrative of Tony Bellew's career, highlighting his resilience, versatility across weight classes, and his ability to deliver thrilling performances on the big stage. These iconic matchups cemented Bellew's legacy as a formidable and entertaining figure in the world of boxing.

CHAPTER 10: Boxing Commentator

Tony Bellew seamlessly transitioned into a role as a boxing commentator, leveraging his extensive experience in the sport and his articulate communication style. As a boxing commentator, Bellew contributed to the broadcast and analysis of live boxing matches, providing insights and observations to enhance the viewer's understanding and enjoyment of the sport.

Key aspects of Tony Bellew's role as a boxing commentator include:

1. **Expert Analysis:** Bellew brought a unique perspective to the commentary booth, drawing from his firsthand experience as a professional boxer. His expert analysis enriched the commentary, offering viewers insights into the technical aspects of the fights, strategies employed by the boxers, and the dynamics within the ring.

Tony bellew

2. **Fighter's Insight:** Given his background, Bellew was able to provide a fighter's insight into the mental and emotional aspects of high-stakes bouts. This added depth to the commentary, giving viewers a glimpse into the mindset of the athletes in the ring.

3. **Articulate Communication:** Bellew's articulate communication style made him effective in conveying complex aspects of boxing in a clear and engaging manner. Whether breaking down technical elements or narrating the ebb and flow of a match, he communicated with precision and enthusiasm.

4. **Collaboration with Broadcast Team:** Bellew worked collaboratively with the broadcast team, including fellow commentators, analysts, and hosts. His ability to seamlessly integrate into the team contributed to the overall quality of the broadcast.

5. **Adaptability:** Bellew's adaptability as a commentator allowed him to cover a range of fights across different weight classes and styles. His versatility

ensured that he could provide relevant insights irrespective of the specific characteristics of each match.

6. **Audience Connection:** Bellew's engaging personality and passion for the sport resonated with the audience. His ability to connect with viewers, whether seasoned boxing fans or casual observers, added a relatable and human element to the commentary.

7. **Post-Fight Analysis:** Beyond the live action, Bellew often participated in post-fight analysis segments. These discussions allowed him to reflect on the outcomes, assess the strategies employed by the fighters, and provide a comprehensive review of the matches.

Tony Bellew's transition to a boxing commentator showcased not only his expertise in the sport but also his ability to communicate effectively and enhance the viewing experience for audiences tuning in to watch live boxing events.

CHAPTER 11: Fighter's Insight

Tony Bellew's fighter's insight as a boxing commentator offered viewers a unique perspective into the intricate world of professional boxing. Here are key elements of Bellew's fighter's insight:

1. **Technical Analysis:** Bellew, drawing from his experience as a professional boxer, provided technical analysis of the fights. This included breakdowns of boxing techniques, footwork, defensive strategies, and offensive tactics employed by the fighters in the ring.

2. **Ringcraft Understanding:** His fighter's insight extended to a deep understanding of ringcraft. Bellew shared observations about how fighters navigated the space, controlled the distance, and strategically positioned themselves to gain advantages over their opponents.

3. **Mental and Emotional Dynamics:** Bellew delved into the mental and emotional dynamics of boxing, offering commentary on the mindset of fighters during high-pressure situations. His insights provided viewers with a glimpse into the psychological aspects of the sport, including resilience, determination, and strategic thinking.

4. **Strategic Approaches:** Bellew analyzed the strategic approaches adopted by fighters, shedding light on their game plans, adjustments during the course of a match, and the execution of specific tactics to exploit an opponent's weaknesses.

5. **Fighter's Preparation:** Bellew's commentary often touched on the preparation that goes into a professional boxing bout. This included insights into training regimens, sparring sessions, and the physical and mental conditioning required for fighters to perform at their best on fight night.

6. **Corner and Coaching Dynamics:** Bellew's expertise allowed him to analyze the role of corners and coaches during fights. He provided commentary on the instructions given to fighters between rounds, strategic advice offered by coaches, and the impact of corner dynamics on the overall fight strategy.

7. **Impact of Styles:** Recognizing the diversity in boxing styles, Bellew discussed how different styles influenced the dynamics of a fight. Whether contrasting styles clashed or complementary styles created intriguing matchups, he articulated how these factors shaped the course of the bout.

8. **Personal Experience Narratives:** Occasionally, Bellew shared personal anecdotes and narratives from his own career, offering viewers a firsthand account of the challenges and decisions a professional boxer faces in the ring.

Bellew's fighter's insight went beyond the surface-level observations, providing viewers with a comprehensive

Tony bellew

understanding of the technical, tactical, and
psychological elements that make professional boxing a
captivating and nuanced sport. His ability to articulate
these insights enriched the commentary and enhanced
the overall viewing experience for boxing enthusiasts.

CHAPTER 12: Legacy in Boxing

Tony Bellew's legacy in boxing is marked by a combination of achievements, resilience, and contributions to the sport. Here are key elements that contribute to Tony Bellew's lasting legacy in the world of boxing:

1. **World Titles and Championships:** Bellew's journey to becoming a world champion in the cruiserweight division, capturing the WBC title, stands as a defining achievement in his career. His success at the highest level of the sport solidified his place among the elite in his weight class.

2. **Versatility Across Weight Classes:** Bellew's ability to move across different weight classes showcased his versatility as a fighter. Competing in both the light-heavyweight and heavyweight divisions, he

demonstrated his skill and adaptability against a diverse range of opponents.

3. **Iconic Bouts and Victories:** Bellew's victories in iconic bouts, such as those against Nathan Cleverly, David Haye, and Ilunga Makabu, contributed significantly to his legacy. These high-profile wins showcased his talent, resilience, and ability to perform under pressure.

4. **Transition to Acting:** Beyond his accomplishments in the ring, Bellew's successful transition to acting added a unique dimension to his legacy. His roles in films like "Creed" highlighted his ability to excel outside of boxing, expanding his influence beyond the sport.

5. **Fighter's Insight as a Commentator:** Bellew's role as a boxing commentator allowed him to share his insights and expertise with a global audience. His articulate commentary and fighter's perspective

enhanced the viewing experience for fans, contributing to his impact on the sport even after retirement.

6. **Liverpool's Boxing Heritage:** Hailing from Liverpool, Bellew became a part of the city's rich boxing heritage. His achievements and contributions added to the legacy of Liverpool's boxing tradition, earning him recognition as a local hero.

7. **Resilience in the Face of Challenges:** Bellew's career was marked by resilience in the face of challenges. Overcoming setbacks, taking on formidable opponents, and bouncing back from defeats showcased his tenacity and determination, leaving an indelible mark on his legacy.

8. **Charitable and Community Contributions:** Bellew's involvement in charitable and community initiatives demonstrated his commitment to giving back. His contributions to various causes outside of the ring added a philanthropic dimension to his legacy, reflecting

a sense of responsibility beyond his athletic achievements.

9. **Fan Connection and Popularity:** Bellew's engaging personality and connection with fans contributed to his enduring popularity. His ability to resonate with a broad audience, both within and outside the boxing community, cemented his status as a beloved figure in the sport.

Tony Bellew's legacy is a multifaceted tapestry that goes beyond titles and victories. It encompasses his versatility, resilience, contributions to boxing culture, and the impact he continues to make in various spheres. As the echoes of his career reverberate through the boxing world, Tony Bellew stands as a testament to the enduring legacy of a true pugilistic artist.

CHAPTER 12: Outside the Ring

Outside the ring, Tony Bellew's life is characterized by various facets that showcase his personality, interests, and contributions beyond the realm of professional boxing:

1. **Acting Career:** Bellew made a successful transition to acting, taking on roles in films such as "Creed" (2015) and its sequel "Creed II" (2018). His foray into the world of entertainment demonstrated his versatility and ability to excel in diverse fields.

2. **Media Personality:** Beyond his commentary roles, Bellew became a recognizable media personality. His appearances on television programs, radio shows, podcasts, and interviews allowed him to connect with audiences, sharing his insights and experiences beyond the boxing ring.

3. **Public Speaker:** Bellew engaged in public speaking engagements, sharing motivational messages and insights from his boxing journey. His ability to articulate lessons learned from his career made him a sought-after speaker at various events.

4. **Community Engagement:** Committed to his community, Bellew participated in charitable initiatives and community outreach programs. His efforts to give back reflected a sense of social responsibility and a desire to make a positive impact beyond his athletic achievements.

5. **Family Life:** Bellew often shared glimpses of his family life, emphasizing the importance of his roles as a husband and father. This aspect added a personal touch to his public image, showcasing a balance between the demands of his career and his family commitments.

6. **Fitness and Well-being:** Post-retirement, Bellew maintained a focus on fitness and well-being. Sharing

aspects of his training routines and promoting a healthy lifestyle, he continued to inspire others to prioritize physical fitness.

7. **Entertainment Industry Involvement:** In addition to acting, Bellew explored various aspects of the entertainment industry. Whether making guest appearances on entertainment shows or participating in projects outside the ring, he expanded his presence in the cultural landscape.

8. **Entrepreneurial Ventures:** Bellew ventured into entrepreneurial pursuits, leveraging his brand and profile. Whether through endorsements, business ventures, or collaborations, he demonstrated a business-minded approach to his post-boxing career.

9. **Fan Interaction:** Bellew maintained an active presence on social media, engaging with fans and providing updates on his endeavors. This direct interaction allowed him to connect with a global audience and foster a supportive fanbase.

Tony bellew

Tony Bellew's life outside the ring is a dynamic tapestry that encompasses entertainment, community engagement, family values, and a commitment to personal growth. His ability to navigate and succeed in various spheres speaks to his adaptability and the enduring impact he continues to make beyond his storied boxing career.

Tony bellew

CHAPTER 13: Tony Bellew: The Art of Boxing Brilliance - Mastering the Sweet Science Inside and Outside the Ring

"Tony Bellew: The Art of Boxing Brilliance - Mastering the Sweet Science Inside and Outside the Ring" is a title that reflects on the comprehensive journey of Tony Bellew, both as a pugilist and as a multifaceted individual. This book dives into the intricate world of boxing brilliance, exploring the nuances of his career and the layers that define his legacy:

1. **Origins and Ascent:** Uncover the origins of Tony Bellew's boxing journey, from his early days in Liverpool to the ascent that led him to championship glory. Delve into the roots that shaped his character and determination in the sweet science.

2. **Versatility Across Weight Classes:** Explore Bellew's unparalleled versatility as he navigated through different weight classes, leaving an indelible mark in each division. Witness the strategic brilliance behind his

decisions and the challenges he embraced to become a force in multiple arenas.

3. **Iconic Bouts:** Relive the thrilling moments of Bellew's iconic bouts, from the heart-pounding victories to the dramatic encounters that defined his career. Each chapter unfolds the narratives behind these battles, showcasing the artistry and brilliance within the boxing ring.

4. **Beyond Boxing: Acting and Entertainment:** Step into the world beyond the ring as Bellew transitions seamlessly into acting and the entertainment industry. Unearth the details of his ventures in Hollywood and the artistic brilliance that extends beyond the confines of a boxing match.

5. **Media Roles and Commentary Brilliance:** Gain insights into Bellew's role as a boxing commentator, where his articulate brilliance brought a fighter's perspective to the commentary booth. Explore how he

elevated the viewing experience for audiences, blending technical analysis with a deep love for the sport.

6. **Life Outside the Ring:** Peel back the layers of Tony Bellew's life outside the ring, from his family dynamics to community engagement and entrepreneurial ventures. Understand the essence of the man behind the gloves and his contributions to various facets of life beyond the boxing arena.

7. **Legacy and Impact:** Reflect on the enduring legacy of Tony Bellew and the impact he has made on the sport of boxing. Evaluate the broader influence he continues to exert as a role model, speaker, and ambassador for the sweet science.

In "Tony Bellew: The Art of Boxing Brilliance," readers will embark on a comprehensive journey that goes beyond the standard boxing biography. This book seeks to capture the brilliance of a man who mastered the sweet science inside and outside the ring, leaving an indelible imprint on the canvas of boxing history.

Tony bellew

CHAPTER 14: Reflection and Legacy

"Tony Bellew: Reflection and Legacy" is a poignant exploration into the profound impact and lasting imprint left by the accomplished boxer. This book delves into the reflections of his storied career and the legacy he crafted, both inside and outside the boxing ring:

1. **Early Reflections:** Begin with Tony Bellew's early reflections, tracing the roots of his boxing journey. Uncover the motivations, challenges, and pivotal moments that shaped the aspiring pugilist before he entered the professional arena.

2. **Championship Aspirations:** Explore Bellew's journey to championship glory, reliving the highs and lows of his pursuit. Gain insights into the mindset, training, and strategic brilliance that fueled his ascent to becoming a world-class boxer.

3. **Iconic Bouts:** Revisit the iconic bouts that defined Bellew's career. Analyze the brilliance displayed in each match, from tactical triumphs to heart-pounding victories, and understand the narratives that contributed to his legacy.

4. **Versatility Across Weight Classes:** Reflect on Bellew's exceptional versatility as he transcended weight classes, showcasing his adaptability and skill across different divisions. Witness the strategic brilliance that allowed him to excel in multiple realms of professional boxing.

5. **Beyond Boxing Brilliance:** Delve into Bellew's endeavors beyond the boxing ring, including his successful foray into acting and entertainment. Understand the brilliance that characterized his pursuits outside the sport, showcasing a multifaceted individual with talents extending far beyond the squared circle.

6. **Legacy in the Community:** Assess Bellew's impact on the community through charitable contributions and community engagement. Explore the ways in which he used his platform to make a positive difference, leaving a lasting legacy beyond the confines of competitive boxing.

7. **Media Roles and Insightful Commentary:** Reflect on Bellew's transition to media roles and his insightful commentary as a boxing analyst. Understand how his unique perspective added depth to the viewing experience, offering fans a fighter's insight into the sweet science.

8. **Personal Reflections:** Gain intimate insights into Tony Bellew's personal reflections on his journey. Explore his thoughts on resilience, setbacks, triumphs, and the valuable lessons learned throughout his career.

9. **Enduring Popularity and Fan Connection:** Reflect on Bellew's enduring popularity and the strong connection he maintained with fans. Analyze the factors

that endeared him to audiences worldwide and contributed to the longevity of his influence in the world of sports.

10. **Legacy Beyond the Ring:** Conclude with an exploration of Tony Bellew's enduring legacy, evaluating the impact he continues to make in the realms of sports, entertainment, and beyond. Assess the broader significance of his story and the mark he leaves on the sweet science.

"Tony Bellew: Reflection and Legacy" provides readers with a comprehensive and introspective journey, inviting them to reflect on the brilliance of a boxer whose legacy extends far beyond the boundaries of the boxing ring.

CHAPTER 14: In His Own Words

"In His Own Words: The Tony Bellew Story" offers an intimate and authentic exploration into the life, career, and reflections of the renowned boxer. This book, presented through Bellew's own words, provides readers with a firsthand account of his journey, triumphs, challenges, and the lessons learned along the way:

1. **Origins and Ambitions:** Begin with Tony Bellew's personal account of his origins, growing up in Liverpool, and the early ambitions that sparked his interest in boxing. Explore the roots of his passion for the sweet science.

2. **Amateur Beginnings:** Hear Bellew's narrative of his amateur boxing days, detailing the challenges and triumphs that shaped his formative years in the sport.

Tony bellew

Gain insights into the early experiences that laid the foundation for his professional career.

3. **Professional Ascent:** Experience the highs and lows of Bellew's professional ascent, from the local circuits to the global stage. Walk alongside him through pivotal fights, victories, and the determination that fueled his pursuit of championship titles.

4. **Versatility Across Weight Classes:** Understand, in his own words, the strategic brilliance behind his decision to move across different weight classes. Explore the challenges and triumphs as he showcased his adaptability against a diverse array of opponents.

5. **Iconic Bouts:** Relive the most memorable moments of Bellew's career through his vivid recollections of iconic bouts. Get a ringside view of the drama, strategy, and emotions that defined these critical junctures in his journey.

6. **Transition to Acting and Beyond:** Listen to Bellew's reflections on his transition to acting and his ventures beyond the boxing ring. Understand the motivations and experiences that led him to explore new realms in the entertainment industry.

7. **Life Outside the Ring:** Gain personal insights into Bellew's life outside the ring, including his family, community engagement, and personal values. Explore the aspects that define him beyond the title of a professional athlete.

8. **Media Roles and Commentary:** Learn about Bellew's experiences as a boxing commentator and media personality. Hear his thoughts on providing insights, connecting with audiences, and contributing to the boxing community in a different capacity.

9. **Legacy and Reflections:** Reflect alongside Bellew on the legacy he leaves behind and the impact he hopes to make. Hear his personal reflections on

resilience, growth, and the enduring connection with fans around the world.

10. **Future Aspirations:** Conclude with Bellew's thoughts on his future aspirations, both within and outside the realm of boxing. Explore his vision for the next chapter and the contributions he envisions making in the years to come.

"In His Own Words: The Tony Bellew Story" offers readers an authentic and unfiltered journey into the heart and mind of a champion, allowing them to connect with the man behind the gloves and experience his narrative firsthand

In Tony Bellew's own words, his future aspirations reflect a blend of personal and professional goals, showcasing a multifaceted individual with ambitions that extend beyond his illustrious boxing career:

1. **Continued Impact in Boxing:** Bellew expresses a desire to continue contributing to the world of boxing.

Tony bellew

Whether through commentary, analysis, or mentorship, he envisions playing a role in shaping the future of the sport and supporting the next generation of fighters.

2. **Promoting Health and Fitness:** With a strong commitment to fitness and well-being, Bellew aspires to promote a healthy lifestyle. He envisions encouraging individuals to prioritize physical fitness, drawing on his own experiences to inspire others to embrace the benefits of an active and balanced life.

3. **Community Engagement:** Building on his history of community involvement, Bellew expresses a continued dedication to charitable initiatives and community engagement. He sees himself leveraging his platform to make a positive impact in the lives of those who may benefit from his influence.

4. **Entrepreneurial Ventures:** Bellew's entrepreneurial spirit shines through as he envisions exploring business ventures and projects beyond the realm of sports and entertainment. Whether through

endorsements, partnerships, or personal ventures, he aims to diversify his portfolio and explore new opportunities.

5. **Family Focus:** Family remains a central theme in Bellew's future aspirations. He emphasizes the importance of maintaining a balance between his professional endeavors and family life, cherishing the roles of husband and father as integral aspects of his identity.

6. **Media Presence:** Bellew sees a continued presence in the media landscape, contributing his insights and perspectives on boxing and beyond. Whether through television appearances, interviews, or other media platforms, he aims to stay connected with audiences worldwide.

7. **Motivational Speaking:** Leveraging his experiences and the lessons learned throughout his career, Bellew expresses an interest in motivational speaking. He envisions sharing his journey, insights, and

Tony bellew

motivational messages to inspire and uplift individuals facing challenges in various aspects of life.

8. **Global Impact:** Beyond local and regional spheres, Bellew aspires to have a global impact. Whether through international engagements, collaborations, or initiatives, he envisions extending his influence to connect with audiences on a broader scale.

9. **Creative Pursuits:** Building on his success in acting, Bellew expresses an interest in exploring further creative pursuits. Whether in film, television, or other artistic endeavors, he envisions tapping into his creative side and embracing new challenges in the entertainment industry.

10. **Legacy of Positivity:** Ultimately, Bellew articulates a desire to leave a legacy characterized by positivity. He aspires to be remembered not only for his accomplishments in the ring but also for the positive contributions he makes to various facets of life, leaving a lasting imprint on the world.

Tony bellew

Tony Bellew's future aspirations reflect a man driven by a diverse range of goals, blending his passion for sports, fitness, family, entrepreneurship, and making a positive impact on a global scale. As he transitions into the next phase of his journey, Bellew's vision extends far beyond the boundaries of a boxing ring.

CHAPTER 15: Tony Bellew: Knuckles and Heart

"Tony Bellew: Knuckles and Heart" is a title that encapsulates the essence of the renowned boxer's journey, emphasizing the grit, determination, and passion that define his career both inside and outside the ring. This book delves into the compelling narrative of Bellew's life, showcasing the balance between the toughness of his knuckles and the depth of his heart:

1. **Bare-Knuckle Beginnings:** Explore the early chapters of Bellew's life, from his humble beginnings to the gritty environments that forged the foundation of his character. Uncover the raw, bare-knuckle origins that set the stage for his rise in the world of professional boxing.

2. **Heart of a Fighter:** Delve into the heart of Tony Bellew, examining the emotional and mental fortitude

that fueled his journey to becoming a champion. Explore the moments of adversity, resilience, and unwavering determination that showcased the true heart of a fighter.

3. **Iconic Knuckle Clashes:** Revisit the iconic clashes where Bellew's knuckles spoke volumes in the ring. Analyze the strategic brilliance, power, and technical prowess that marked his battles against formidable opponents, leaving an indelible imprint on the landscape of professional boxing.

4. **Family Ties and Heartfelt Connections:** Unwind the layers of Bellew's personal life, exploring the significance of family ties and heartfelt connections. Witness the impact of his heart not only on his professional journey but also in the relationships that define him beyond the realm of sports.

5. **Heartfelt Victories and Defeats:** Reflect on the heartfelt victories and defeats that shaped Bellew's career. Each triumph and setback becomes a chapter in the story of a fighter who poured his heart into every

moment, leaving an enduring legacy in the annals of boxing history.

6. **Community Engagement with a Knuckled Purpose:** Understand the connection between Bellew's knuckles and his commitment to community engagement. Explore the charitable initiatives, impactful projects, and contributions that reflect his dedication to making a positive impact beyond the confines of the ring.

7. **Media Roles: Articulating with Knuckle Precision:** Analyze Bellew's transition to media roles, where he articulates with knuckle precision as a boxing commentator. Witness how his sharp insights and articulate commentary provide audiences with a ringside perspective, enhancing the viewing experience.

8. **Knuckles in the Entertainment Spotlight:** Step into the entertainment spotlight with Bellew as he showcases his knuckles in various creative pursuits. From acting roles to entrepreneurial ventures, explore

Tony bellew

how his knuckles extend beyond the physical realm into diverse aspects of the entertainment industry.

"Tony Bellew: Knuckles and Heart" invites readers to witness the fusion of toughness and compassion that defines a boxer who not only fought with knuckles of steel but also showcased a heart full of passion, resilience, and humanity throughout his extraordinary journey.

CHAPTER 16: Heartfelt Victories and Defeats

In the realm of Tony Bellew's career, each victory and defeat is a chapter in a compelling story, reflecting the heartfelt moments that defined his journey inside and outside the boxing ring:

1. **Triumph Over Edison Miranda (2012):** Bellew's victory over Edison Miranda marked a pivotal moment. The heartfelt triumph showcased his determination, technical skill, and ability to overcome challenges, setting the stage for greater achievements in his career.

2. **Redemption Against Nathan Cleverly II (2014):** In a heartfelt rematch, Bellew sought redemption against Nathan Cleverly. The victory not only secured the WBA (Regular) light-heavyweight title but also symbolized resilience and the ability to turn setbacks into triumphs.

3. **Cruiserweight Glory vs. Ilunga Makabu (2016):**
One of the most emotional victories came in the
cruiserweight division. Bellew's knockout win against
Ilunga Makabu at Goodison Park fulfilled a lifelong
dream, bringing tears of joy and underscoring the
heartfelt connection between a boxer and his aspirations.

4. **David Haye Duology (2017, 2018):** The heartfelt
victories over David Haye in two intense bouts
showcased Bellew's ability to defy odds. Overcoming
adversity, he displayed both skill and heart, earning
respect and solidifying his status as a formidable force in
the heavyweight division.

5. **Undisputed Cruiserweight Challenge vs. Oleksandr
Usyk (2018):** While the result was a defeat, the
heartfelt battle against Oleksandr Usyk for the
undisputed cruiserweight title demonstrated Bellew's
courage and willingness to face the very best. The
emotional journey of that bout left an indelible mark on
his legacy.

6. **Heartbreaking Loss to Adonis Stevenson (2013):**
The defeat to Adonis Stevenson was a poignant moment in Bellew's career. The heartfelt loss fueled his determination for redemption and highlighted the emotional toll that comes with the pursuit of greatness in the sport.

7. **Farewell Bout vs. Oleksandr Usyk (2018):**
Bellew's final bout, a heartfelt farewell against Usyk, showcased his dedication and the emotional complexity of stepping away from the sport he loved. It was a poignant moment that marked the end of an era in his boxing journey.

8. **Balancing Wins and Losses with Emotional Resilience:** Throughout his career, Bellew's ability to balance victories and defeats with emotional resilience defined his character. The heartfelt nature of each bout, whether a win or a loss, reflected a fighter who invested his emotions and passion into every performance.

Tony bellew

These heartfelt victories and defeats collectively form the tapestry of Tony Bellew's boxing legacy, portraying not just the physical prowess of a champion but the emotional depth of a man who lived and breathed the sweet science. Each moment is a testament to his heart, courage, and the indomitable spirit that defined his remarkable career.

CHAPTER 17: Fan Interaction

Tony Bellew's fan interaction has been a hallmark of his career, characterized by genuine connection, appreciation, and a strong bond with those who supported him. Here are key aspects of Tony Bellew's fan interaction:

1. **Accessible on Social Media:** Bellew maintained an active presence on social media platforms, providing fans with direct access to his thoughts, updates, and behind-the-scenes glimpses of his life. This accessibility allowed fans to feel closely connected to his journey.

2. **Acknowledging Support:** Bellew consistently acknowledged and expressed gratitude for the support he received from fans. Whether through post-fight interviews, social media posts, or public appearances, he

made it a point to recognize the importance of fan support in his career.

3. **Engaging with Supporters:** During public events, Bellew engaged with fans by signing autographs, posing for photos, and taking the time to converse with those who admired his work. This personal touch endeared him to supporters, creating lasting memories for those fortunate enough to meet him.

4. **Fan-Centric Approach in Media:** In media interviews and appearances, Bellew often spoke directly to fans. His messages were crafted with the audience in mind, acknowledging the role fans played in fueling his motivation and contributing to the overall spectacle of professional boxing.

5. **Openness and Transparency:** Bellew's openness and transparency in sharing his journey resonated with fans. From discussing victories to addressing setbacks, he allowed fans a glimpse into the emotional highs and lows of a professional boxer's life.

6. **Interacting at Boxing Events:** Whether before or after matches, Bellew engaged with fans at boxing events. His willingness to connect with the audience, share moments of triumph or reflection, and sign memorabilia created a sense of shared experience with those who followed his career.

7. **Fan-Centric Initiatives:** Bellew participated in fan-centric initiatives, including giveaways, contests, and interactive sessions. These efforts demonstrated his commitment to creating memorable experiences for supporters and fostering a sense of community within his fan base.

8. **Responding to Fan Messages:** Despite his busy schedule, Bellew made an effort to respond to fan messages and comments on social media. This direct engagement further strengthened the connection between him and those who admired his skills and personality.

Tony bellew

9. **Appreciation for Local Support:** Hailing from Liverpool, Bellew had a deep appreciation for the support he received from his local community. He often acknowledged the significance of his roots and the pride he felt in representing Liverpool in the world of boxing.

Tony Bellew's fan interaction was marked by authenticity and a genuine appreciation for those who supported him. His ability to connect with fans on a personal level contributed to the enduring popularity and admiration he garnered throughout his career.

CHAPTER 18: Transition to Acting

Tony Bellew's transition to acting marked a successful and notable expansion of his career beyond the boxing ring. Here are key aspects of his journey into the world of acting:

1. **Film Debut in "Creed" (2015):** Bellew made a significant impact in Hollywood with his debut role in the film "Creed," a part of the iconic "Rocky" film series. His portrayal of the character "Pretty" Ricky Conlan showcased not only his physical presence but also his ability to convey emotion on the big screen.

2. **Recognition for Acting Prowess:** Bellew received praise for his performance in "Creed," with critics and audiences acknowledging his natural screen presence and authenticity as an actor. His success in the film marked a promising start to his acting career.

3. **Sequel "Creed II" (2018):** Bellew reprised his role in the sequel, "Creed II," further solidifying his place in the film franchise. His involvement in the series demonstrated a continued commitment to the craft of acting and an eagerness to explore the evolution of his character.

4. **Diverse Acting Roles:** Beyond the "Creed" series, Bellew explored diverse acting roles in both film and television. This versatility allowed him to showcase his range as an actor, taking on characters that went beyond the realm of his boxing persona.

5. **Collaboration with Accomplished Actors:** Bellew had the opportunity to work alongside accomplished actors in the industry. Collaborating with seasoned professionals provided him with valuable learning experiences and contributed to the growth of his acting skills.

6. **Smooth Transition from Boxing to Acting:**
Bellew's transition from boxing to acting was notable for
its smoothness. His ability to navigate the complexities
of two distinct worlds demonstrated not only his physical
prowess but also his adaptability and dedication to
honing new skills.

7. **Positive Reception from Industry Peers:** Within
the entertainment industry, Bellew received positive
recognition from peers and industry insiders for his
commitment to acting. This acknowledgment helped
solidify his status as a credible and respected presence in
Hollywood.

8. **Entrepreneurial Ventures in Entertainment:**
Beyond acting roles, Bellew explored entrepreneurial
ventures within the entertainment industry. This included
potential collaborations, business endeavors, or projects
that allowed him to leverage his profile and expertise
gained from his acting career.

Tony bellew

Tony Bellew's transition to acting showcased his ability to seamlessly transition from one demanding profession to another. His success in Hollywood not only expanded his reach and influence but also demonstrated his capacity to excel in diverse and challenging creative pursuits.

CHAPTER 19: Tony Bellew: A Puncher's Path

"Tony Bellew: A Puncher's Path" is a title that encapsulates the compelling journey of the renowned boxer, emphasizing the strategic and powerful nature of his career. This book explores key elements along Bellew's path, from his humble beginnings to the pinnacle of success:

1. **Origins in Liverpool:** Begin by tracing Tony Bellew's origins in Liverpool, exploring the environments that shaped his character and instilled in him the attributes of a natural puncher. The vibrant city becomes the backdrop for the early chapters of his story.

2. **Amateur Aspirations:** Dive into Bellew's aspirations in the amateur boxing circuit. Explore the

early development of his punching prowess, highlighting the dedication, training, and formative experiences that laid the foundation for his professional career.

3. **Professional Ascent:** Navigate through Bellew's professional ascent, witnessing the calculated path he carved through various weight classes. Explore the progression of his punching power and the strategic brilliance that propelled him to championship status.

4. **Iconic Punching Moments:** Relive the most iconic punching moments in Bellew's career. From devastating knockouts to powerful blows that defined crucial matches, each moment becomes a chapter, showcasing the artistry and impact of a true puncher.

5. **Heartfelt Battles:** Explore the heartfelt battles where Bellew's punching power was put to the test. Whether in victories or defeats, these chapters unravel the emotional depth behind each powerful punch and its significance in his journey.

6. **Versatility in Punching Styles:** Delve into the versatility of Bellew's punching styles. From precision jabs to powerful hooks, analyze the technical aspects that made his punching approach dynamic and adaptable to different opponents.

7. **David Haye Duology:** Spotlight the duology against David Haye, where Bellew's punching power played a pivotal role. Analyze the technical brilliance and strategic punches that led to triumphs in two high-stakes and emotionally charged bouts.

8. **Punching Precision Beyond Boxing:** Explore how Bellew's punching precision extended beyond the boxing ring. Whether in media commentary, acting roles, or entrepreneurial ventures, witness how his calculated punches transcended the physical realm into various aspects of his career.

9. **Impact Beyond the Ring:** Reflect on the impact of Bellew's punches beyond the boxing ring. From charitable endeavors to community engagement, analyze

how his influence and powerful punches contributed to making a positive impact in the lives of others.

10. **Legacy of a Puncher:** Conclude with an exploration of Tony Bellew's legacy as a puncher. Assess the lasting impact of his punching prowess on the sport of boxing, his fans, and the indelible mark he leaves on the canvas of pugilistic history.

"Tony Bellew: A Puncher's Path" offers readers a ringside seat to the powerful and strategic journey of a true puncher, showcasing the art, science, and impact of Bellew's distinguished career.

CHAPTER 20: Heartfelt Battles

"Heartfelt Battles" in Tony Bellew's career are chapters filled with emotional intensity, resilience, and the profound impact of facing formidable opponents. Here are some key moments that define these heartfelt battles:

1. **Nathan Cleverly Rivalry (2011, 2014):** The battles against Nathan Cleverly were more than just sporting contests; they were personal and emotionally charged. The heartfelt nature of these encounters added layers to their rivalry, culminating in Bellew's redemption victory in the rematch.

2. **Adonis Stevenson Showdown (2013):** The bout against Adonis Stevenson was a heartfelt battle that showcased Bellew's courage and determination. Despite facing defeat, the emotional toll and the lessons learned

from this match fueled his pursuit of greatness in the light heavyweight division.

3. **Ilunga Makabu: Cruiserweight Dream Realized (2016):** The cruiserweight clash against Ilunga Makabu was a heartfelt battle that transcended the typical quest for a title. The emotional resonance came from Bellew fulfilling a lifelong dream of becoming a world champion in his hometown of Liverpool.

4. **David Haye Duology (2017, 2018):** The two encounters with David Haye were emotionally charged and symbolic of Bellew's journey. The heartfelt battles against the former heavyweight champion showcased Bellew's resilience, strategy, and determination to overcome adversity.

5. **Undisputed Cruiserweight Challenge vs. Oleksandr Usyk (2018):** The challenge for the undisputed cruiserweight title against Oleksandr Usyk was a poignant moment in Bellew's career. The heartfelt battle

represented his willingness to face the very best, even in the face of defeat, leaving a lasting impact on his legacy.

6. **Farewell Bout Against Oleksandr Usyk (2018):** The final bout against Usyk was not just a farewell; it was a heartfelt goodbye to the sport. Emotions ran high as Bellew left everything in the ring, capping off a remarkable career with a bout that encapsulated the passion and heart he brought to boxing.

7. **Balancing Heartfelt Victories and Losses:** Throughout his career, Bellew's battles were not only about victories but also about navigating the emotional landscape of defeats. The heartfelt nature of each outcome, whether a triumph or setback, defined his character and resilience.

8. **Legacy of Heart and Grit:** Bellew's legacy is not just about titles but about the heart he displayed in the ring. The heartfelt battles collectively contribute to a legacy built on resilience, determination, and the emotional journey of a fighter who gave his all.

Tony bellew

These heartfelt battles in Tony Bellew's career go beyond the physicality of the sport, revealing the emotional and human elements that make boxing a deeply personal journey. Each battle, win or lose, added layers to his narrative, leaving an indelible mark on the hearts of fans and the history of the sweet science.

CHAPTER 21:Legacy of Heart and Grit

Tony Bellew's legacy is one of heart and grit, defined by the unwavering determination, resilience, and passion he brought to the sport of boxing. Here are key elements that contribute to his enduring legacy:

1. **Resilience in the Face of Adversity:** Bellew's legacy is marked by his ability to bounce back from setbacks. Whether facing defeats or overcoming personal challenges, his resilience became a defining characteristic, earning him admiration from fans and peers alike.

2. **Heartfelt Victories:** Bellew's legacy is enriched by the heartfelt victories he secured throughout his career. Each triumph represented not only technical skill but also a display of heart   an unyiclding spirit that

propelled him to overcome formidable opponents and achieve championship glory.

3. **Emotional Connections with Fans:** The emotional connections Bellew forged with fans contribute significantly to his legacy. His accessibility, authenticity, and gratitude toward his supporters created a bond that extended beyond the boxing ring, making him a beloved figure in the world of sports.

4. **Courage in Pursuit of Dreams:** Bellew's legacy is intertwined with the courage he exhibited in pursuing his dreams. From his early days in Liverpool to achieving success on the global stage, his fearless pursuit of greatness resonates as a testament to the power of determination and self-belief.

5. **Heart-on-Sleeve Approach:** Known for wearing his heart on his sleeve, Bellew's transparent approach endeared him to fans. His candid expressions of joy, frustration, and determination added depth to his

persona, creating a genuine connection with those who followed his journey.

6. **Versatility Across Weight Classes:** Bellew's legacy is characterized by his versatility in moving across weight classes. His ability to adapt and succeed in different divisions showcased not only his technical skills but also the heart to take on new challenges and conquer uncharted territories.

7. **Symbolic Victories Against the Odds:** Bellew's legacy is punctuated by symbolic victories against opponents considered formidable or favored. These triumphs underscore his ability to overcome odds, proving that heart and grit can be potent weapons inside the ring.

8. **Lasting Impact Beyond Boxing:** Beyond the sport itself, Bellew's legacy extends to the positive impact he made outside the boxing ring. His involvement in charitable endeavors, community engagement, and the

inspiration he provided to others contribute to a legacy that goes beyond athletic achievements.

9. **Emotional Farewell to Boxing:** The emotional farewell to boxing marked the end of an era for Bellew. His heartfelt goodbye, coupled with a memorable final performance, etched his legacy as a fighter who gave his all until the very end of his career.

10. **Legacy of a Fighter with Heart and Grit:** In the annals of boxing history, Tony Bellew's legacy stands as that of a fighter with heart and grit. It's a legacy that transcends statistics and titles, leaving an enduring imprint on the sport and inspiring future generations of boxers.

Tony Bellew's legacy is a testament to the indomitable spirit of a fighter who approached every bout with heart, faced challenges with grit, and left an everlasting impact on the hearts of fans and the history of boxing.

CHAPTER 22: Punching Precision Beyond Boxing

"Punching Precision Beyond Boxing" explores Tony Bellew's ability to channel his calculated and powerful punches into various aspects of his career beyond the boxing ring. Here are key dimensions where his punching precision made a notable impact:

1. **Media Commentary:** Bellew's transition to media commentary showcased his punching precision in articulating insights and analysis. Whether breaking down a fight, predicting outcomes, or providing technical commentary, his precise observations added depth to the viewer's understanding of the sweet science.

2. **Strategic Business Ventures:** Bellew leveraged his punching precision in strategic business ventures. From endorsements to collaborations, his calculated

Tony bellew

approach extended beyond the ring, contributing to successful entrepreneurial endeavors in the business and entertainment sectors.

3. **Acting Roles:** In his acting roles, Bellew's punching precision manifested in the nuanced portrayal of characters. The ability to deliver lines with precision, convey emotions effectively, and command attention on screen demonstrated a seamless transfer of his skills from the ring to the entertainment industry.

4. **Public Speaking Engagements:** Whether at events, conferences, or public speaking engagements, Bellew's punching precision was evident in his ability to connect with audiences. His articulate delivery, combined with the impactful use of words, showcased a speaker who could command attention and convey messages with precision.

5. **Community Engagement:** Bellew directed his punching precision toward community engagement and charitable initiatives. The strategic allocation of

resources, time, and influence demonstrated a thoughtful approach to making a positive impact beyond the confines of professional boxing.

6. **Entertainment Industry:** Bellew's involvement in the entertainment industry, including roles in film and television, highlighted his ability to bring punching precision to creative pursuits. The calculated decisions in choosing projects and the dedication to delivering compelling performances showcased his multifaceted talents.

7. **Global Influence:** Beyond the local and regional spheres, Bellew's punching precision extended to a global audience. Whether through international collaborations or engagements, he showcased a strategic approach to expanding his influence on a broader scale.

8. **Cross-Industry Collaborations:** Bellew's calculated punches extended to cross-industry collaborations. His ability to collaborate effectively with professionals from diverse fields, including

entertainment, business, and philanthropy, demonstrated an understanding of how punching precision could be applied in varied contexts.

9. **Brand Endorsements:** Bellew's strategic brand endorsements showcased punching precision in aligning with products and organizations that complemented his image. His calculated choices contributed to successful partnerships that extended his reach beyond the boxing community.

10. **Legacy of Precision:** Bellew's legacy includes a lasting impact through the precision with which he approached various aspects of his post-boxing career. Whether as a commentator, actor, entrepreneur, or philanthropist, his legacy of punching precision endures as a testament to a fighter who seamlessly translated his skills into diverse arenas.

"Punching Precision Beyond Boxing" captures Tony Bellew's ability to wield his calculated and powerful punches in a strategic manner, leaving an indelible mark

Tony bellew

not only in the world of sports but across multiple facets
of his post-boxing journey.

CHAPTER 23: Fighter's Insight as a Commentator

Tony Bellew's fighter's insight as a commentator brought a unique perspective to the world of boxing analysis. Here are key aspects that defined his role as a commentator:

1. **Technical Expertise:** Bellew's background as a professional boxer equipped him with unparalleled technical expertise. As a commentator, he provided viewers with in-depth insights into the mechanics of a fight, breaking down techniques, strategies, and the finer nuances that might escape the casual observer.

2. **Ring Psychology:** Bellew's fighter's insight extended beyond the physical aspects of the sport to delve into ring psychology. He could articulate the mental aspects of a bout, explaining the tactical

decisions fighters made and the psychological battles that unfolded during a match.

3. **Strategic Brilliance:** Leveraging his own experiences, Bellew offered strategic brilliance in commentary. Viewers gained a ringside view of the tactical considerations that fighters faced, helping them appreciate the chess match within the ropes.

4. **Emotional Resonance:** Bellew's commentary wasn't just about technicalities; it carried emotional resonance. His passion for the sport and empathy for the fighters allowed him to convey the emotional highs and lows of a bout, making the viewing experience more engaging and relatable.

5. **Instant Analysis:** Known for his ability to provide instant analysis, Bellew could assess unfolding situations in real-time. This skill brought immediacy to his commentary, offering viewers timely and accurate assessments of the action inside the ring.

6. **Connection with Fighters' Journeys:** Having walked the path of a professional boxer, Bellew connected with the journeys of fighters. His commentary reflected an understanding of the sacrifices, challenges, and triumphs that defined the careers of those stepping into the ring.

7. **Balancing Objectivity and Passion:** Bellew achieved a delicate balance between objectivity and passion in his commentary. While providing unbiased analysis, he maintained a genuine enthusiasm for the sport, conveying a deep love for boxing that resonated with viewers.

8. **Clarity in Communication:** Bellew's clarity in communication set him apart. He could translate complex boxing scenarios into easily understandable insights, making the sport more accessible to a broad audience without compromising on the depth of analysis.

9. **Educational Commentary:** Bellew's commentary often served an educational purpose. Whether explaining

specific techniques, strategies, or historical context, he contributed to the audience's boxing education, fostering a deeper appreciation for the intricacies of the sport.

10. **Respected Voice in Boxing:** Over time, Bellew earned respect as a voice in the boxing community. His credibility as a commentator grew, and audiences came to value his opinions and analyses as insightful contributions to the discourse surrounding the sport.

Tony Bellew's fighter's insight as a commentator added a layer of authenticity and depth to boxing broadcasts. His ability to blend technical analysis with emotional storytelling made him a respected and engaging figure in the world of sports commentary.

CHAPTER 24: Instant Analysis

Tony Bellew's ability to provide instant analysis during boxing broadcasts was a hallmark of his commentary style. Here are key elements that defined his talent for immediate and insightful analysis:

1. **Quick Tactical Assessment:** Bellew had a knack for rapidly assessing the tactical dynamics of a fight. Whether analyzing a boxer's footwork, defensive strategies, or offensive maneuvers, he could provide viewers with a clear and concise breakdown of the action as it unfolded.

2. **Strategic Considerations:** Beyond the immediate punches and movements, Bellew delved into the strategic considerations at play. He could decipher a fighter's game plan and highlight pivotal moments that could shape the outcome of the match, all within seconds of the action occurring.

3. **Predictive Insights:** Bellew's instant analysis often extended to predictive insights. Drawing on his own experiences as a boxer, he could anticipate potential strategies, counterattacks, or shifts in momentum, adding an element of foresight to his commentary.

4. **Emotional Impact Assessment:** Recognizing the emotional impact of significant moments, Bellew could instantly convey the gravity of key exchanges. Whether it was a stunning knockout punch or a display of resilience, he articulated the emotional context, enhancing the viewer's connection to the fight.

5. **Adaptability to Fast-Paced Action:** Boxing is a fast-paced sport, and Bellew's ability to adapt to the speed of the action was crucial. His instant analysis demonstrated agility in processing information and conveying insights without missing a beat, enhancing the viewing experience for audiences.

6. **Concise and Clear Communication:** Bellew's instant analysis was characterized by concise and clear communication. In the midst of dynamic rounds, he could distill complex scenarios into easily understandable insights, ensuring that viewers remained engaged and informed.

7. **Balancing Commentary with Play-by-Play:** Whether providing play-by-play narration or stepping into analysis mode, Bellew seamlessly balanced both roles. This versatility allowed him to contribute to the narrative of the fight while offering immediate insights into the technical aspects.

8. **Engaging Audiences in Real-Time:** By offering instant analysis, Bellew engaged audiences in real-time discussions about the unfolding drama in the ring. His commentary became a dynamic and interactive part of the viewing experience, fostering a sense of immediacy and excitement.

9. **Objective Assessment:** Bellew's instant analysis was characterized by objectivity. Even in the heat of intense exchanges, he maintained a composed and unbiased approach, providing fair assessments of the fighters' performances.

10. **Enhancing Broadcast Dynamics:** Bellew's talent for instant analysis contributed to the overall dynamics of boxing broadcasts. His ability to inject timely insights elevated the quality of commentary, making the viewing experience more enriching for both dedicated fans and casual observers.

Tony Bellew's instant analysis not only showcased his deep understanding of the sport but also demonstrated his skill in translating that knowledge into real-time, accessible insights for audiences, enhancing the excitement and appreciation of each bout.

CHAPTER-25 Media Personality

Tony Bellew's transition from the boxing ring to becoming a media personality reflects his versatility and engaging presence. Here are key aspects that define his role as a media personality:

1. **Commentator and Analyst:** As a commentator and analyst, Bellew provided expert insights into boxing matches. His articulate commentary and analytical approach showcased his deep understanding of the sport, making him a valuable voice in the boxing community.

2. **Play-by-Play Narration:** Bellew's ability to offer play-by-play narration added a dynamic element to his media persona. Whether describing the ebb and flow of a fight or capturing the intensity of pivotal moments, he brought a sense of immediacy to viewers.

3. **Expert Panels and Talk Shows:** Bellew frequently participated in expert panels and talk shows, contributing his views on various aspects of boxing. His engaging discussions and candid opinions made him a sought-after personality for discussions on the sport.

4. **Interviewer and Interviewee:** In his media role, Bellew seamlessly transitioned between being an interviewer and interviewee. His charisma and ability to connect with subjects allowed him to conduct compelling interviews, while his own experiences made him an interesting interviewee.

5. **Versatility in Media Genres:** Bellew's media personality extended beyond boxing, showcasing his versatility. He explored diverse media genres, participating in shows that covered entertainment, sports, and lifestyle, demonstrating his ability to engage audiences across different interests.

6. **Social Media Presence:** Bellew maintained an active presence on social media platforms, connecting

with fans and sharing updates about his life beyond boxing. His authenticity and interaction with followers contributed to his media persona's relatability.

7. **Brand Ambassador and Endorsements:** Embracing his media role, Bellew became a brand ambassador for various products and endorsed campaigns. His marketable image and media presence made him a desirable figure for partnerships with brands seeking a connection with the sports audience.

8. **Podcast Host:** Bellew ventured into podcasting, hosting shows where he could delve into in-depth discussions on boxing, sports, and life. His conversational style and ability to bring out engaging narratives added to the appeal of his podcasting endeavors.

9. **Public Speaker:** Leveraging his media personality, Bellew engaged in public speaking engagements. Whether at conferences, events, or motivational talks, he shared his experiences and

insights, captivating audiences with his storytelling prowess.

10. **Crossover into Entertainment:** Bellew's media personality facilitated a crossover into the entertainment industry. His roles in film and television showcased his ability to captivate audiences beyond the realm of sports, further expanding his reach.

Tony Bellew's media personality is characterized by a combination of expertise, charisma, and relatability. His seamless transition from a boxing career to a multifaceted media presence highlights his adaptability and the enduring appeal of his engaging persona.

CHAPTER 26: Public Speaker

Tony Bellew, as a public speaker, brings a dynamic and engaging presence to various events. Here are key aspects that define his role as a public speaker:

1. **Personal Storytelling:** Bellew's public speaking engagements often involve personal storytelling. He shares the compelling narrative of his journey from humble beginnings to becoming a renowned boxer and media personality, resonating with audiences through the power of storytelling.

2. **Motivational Insights:** Leveraging his experiences in the boxing ring, Bellew provides motivational insights. He shares the lessons learned from facing challenges, overcoming setbacks, and achieving success, inspiring audiences to persevere in their own endeavors.

3. **Life Beyond Boxing:** Beyond the ring, Bellew delves into the broader aspects of life. He discusses themes such as resilience, determination, and the importance of embracing opportunities beyond one's comfort zone, offering valuable perspectives applicable to diverse audiences.

4. **Interactive Engagement:** Bellew actively engages with his audience, fostering an interactive and participatory atmosphere. Whether through Q&A sessions, audience interaction, or group discussions, he ensures that the audience feels connected and involved in the conversation.

5. **Candid and Authentic Communication:** Known for his candid and authentic communication style, Bellew's public speaking involves open discussions about both triumphs and challenges. His honesty and transparency create a genuine connection with listeners, making his messages more relatable.

Tony bellew

6. **Leadership and Discipline:** Drawing parallels between boxing and life, Bellew addresses themes of leadership and discipline. He highlights the importance of discipline in achieving goals, emphasizing that the principles learned in the boxing gym can be applied to various aspects of life.

7. **Adaptable Content:** Bellew tailors his content to suit the specific context and objectives of each speaking engagement. Whether addressing corporate audiences, sports enthusiasts, or students, he adapts his messages to resonate with the unique interests and goals of the audience.

8. **Inspiration for Personal Growth:** Through his speeches, Bellew inspires personal growth and development. By sharing how he navigated his own growth, both personally and professionally, he encourages individuals to embrace continuous learning, self-improvement, and the pursuit of excellence.

Tony bellew

9. **Positive Mindset:** Bellew emphasizes the power of a positive mindset in overcoming challenges. His motivational talks often touch on the mental aspect of success, urging listeners to cultivate resilience, focus, and a positive outlook in the face of adversity.

10. **Engaging Presence:** Whether speaking in small gatherings or addressing large audiences, Bellew's engaging presence captivates listeners. His charisma, combined with a natural ability to connect with people, creates an atmosphere where audiences are motivated and inspired.

Tony Bellew's role as a public speaker extends beyond his achievements in boxing, providing audiences with valuable insights, motivation, and a roadmap for personal and professional development. His dynamic speaking style and relatable messages make him a sought-after speaker for a diverse range of events and audiences.

CHAPTER 27: Engaging Presence

Tony Bellew's engaging presence is a distinctive quality that sets him apart in various roles, from boxing to media and public speaking. Here are key elements that contribute to his captivating and relatable presence:

1. **Authenticity:** Bellew's authenticity shines through in his demeanor and communication. Whether in interviews, commentary, or public speaking, he remains true to himself, creating an immediate and genuine connection with audiences.

2. **Expressive Body Language:** His use of expressive body language enhances his engaging presence. From animated gestures to facial expressions, Bellew effectively communicates passion and enthusiasm, making his interactions visually compelling.

3. **Charismatic Communication:** Bellew's charisma is evident in the way he communicates. His tone, inflections, and choice of words convey energy and passion, keeping listeners attentive and responsive to the messages he conveys.

4. **Sense of Humor:** A well-timed sense of humor contributes to Bellew's engaging presence. Whether cracking jokes during interviews or adding light-hearted moments to his commentary, he creates an enjoyable and relatable atmosphere.

5. **Connectivity with the Audience:** Bellew excels in connecting with his audience on a personal level. His ability to read the room, acknowledge the energy of the crowd, and respond to the collective mood ensures that his presence resonates with diverse audiences.

6. **Approachability:** Despite his achievements in boxing, Bellew maintains an approachable demeanor. Whether interacting with fans, fellow athletes, or

colleagues, he exudes an approachability that makes him relatable and likable.

7. **Confident Presence:** Bellew's confidence is a key element of his engaging presence. Whether in the ring, on screen, or in public speaking engagements, his self-assuredness commands attention and instills confidence in those listening to him.

8. **Adaptability:** His engaging presence is adaptable to various contexts. Whether in the intense atmosphere of a boxing match, the analytical setting of commentary, or the more casual environment of interviews, Bellew seamlessly adjusts his presence to suit the occasion.

9. **Empathy:** Bellew's empathetic nature contributes to his engaging presence. His ability to understand and connect with the emotions of others, whether fighters in the ring or audience members, fosters a deeper level of engagement.

10. **Captivating Storytelling:** Whether recounting his own experiences or sharing anecdotes, Bellew's storytelling is captivating. His ability to weave narratives that resonate emotionally with listeners adds depth to his engaging presence.

In every role he undertakes, Tony Bellew's engaging presence is a powerful asset. It transcends the boundaries of sports, making him not only a successful athlete but also a captivating media personality and public speaker whose influence extends to diverse audiences.

CHAPTER 28: Tony Bellew: Ringside Reverie

"Tony Bellew: Ringside Reverie" is a title that encapsulates the reflective and introspective journey of the renowned boxer beyond the ropes. This book delves into the moments of contemplation, self-discovery, and the emotional tapestry that unfolds outside the intense world of professional boxing. Here's a glimpse of what "Ringside Reverie" could encompass:

1. **Introduction to the Arena:** Begin with an exploration of the emotions and thoughts that run through Bellew's mind as he steps into the arena. Set the stage for the reverie by describing the sights, sounds, and palpable energy that define the boxing world.

2. **Echoes of the Past:** Reflect on Bellew's early days in the sport. Uncover the echoes of the past, from

humble beginnings to the challenges and triumphs that shaped his identity and paved the way for a remarkable career.

3. **The Sweet Science Unveiled:** Dive into the intricacies of the sweet science. Explore Bellew's revelations about the art of boxing, detailing the physical and mental demands, the highs of victory, and the lows of defeat.

4. **Inside the Training Camp:** Take readers inside the training camps where the groundwork for success is laid. Capture Bellew's thoughts on discipline, sacrifice, and the relentless pursuit of excellence that defines the preparation for a fight.

5. **In the Spotlight:** Navigate through the moments in the spotlight, from iconic victories to challenging bouts. Unveil Bellew's introspections about the pressures, expectations, and the thrill of being in the center of attention.

Tony bellew

6. **Battles Beyond the Ring:** Explore the personal battles Bellew faced beyond the boxing ring. From the internal struggles to external pressures, delve into the multifaceted nature of his journey as an athlete and a person.

7. **The Impact of Defeat:** Reflect on the impact of defeat on Bellew's mindset. Uncover the resilience and determination that arise in the aftermath of setbacks, shedding light on the transformative power of adversity.

8. **Beyond Boxing: Media Odyssey:** Trace Bellew's journey beyond boxing into the realms of media. Explore his experiences as a commentator, analyst, and media personality, showcasing the evolution of his career beyond the physical demands of the sport.

9. **Life Lessons and Legacy:** Uncover the life lessons Bellew distilled from his experiences. Reflect on the legacy he aimed to leave, both in the sport of boxing and in the broader context of his impact on others.

Tony bellew

10. **The Final Bell:** Conclude with Bellew's contemplation on the final bell of his boxing career. Capture the emotions, reflections, and the sense of fulfillment as he looks back on a career marked by passion, perseverance, and the pursuit of greatness.

"Tony Bellew: Ringside Reverie" offers readers an intimate and introspective journey, providing a ringside seat to the inner workings of a fighter's mind and the reverie that unfolds when the gloves come off.

CHAPTER 29: Life Lessons and Legacy

In "Tony Bellew: Ringside Reverie," the section on life lessons and legacy delves into the profound insights and enduring impact the renowned boxer has garnered throughout his journey. Here are key elements that could be explored in this chapter:

1. **The Power of Perseverance:** Reflect on Bellew's unwavering commitment to his goals. Explore instances where he faced challenges, setbacks, and how his ability to persevere became a guiding principle both inside and outside the ring.

2. **Resilience in the Face of Adversity:** Discuss Bellew's resilience and how he responded to adversity. Highlight specific moments where setbacks became stepping stones, shaping his character and contributing to the resilience that defined his career.

3. **Discipline and Dedication:** Examine the role of discipline and dedication in Bellew's journey. Explore his training routines, sacrifices, and the disciplined approach that played a pivotal role in achieving success in the highly competitive world of professional boxing.

4. **Balancing Ambition and Realism:** Discuss how Bellew navigated the delicate balance between ambitious aspirations and grounded realism. Explore instances where he set high goals but remained realistic, understanding the importance of strategic planning and incremental progress.

5. **Lessons from Defeat:** Reflect on the valuable lessons Bellew gleaned from moments of defeat. Explore how he transformed setbacks into opportunities for growth, learning, and ultimately, how these experiences shaped his resilience and mindset.

6. **Impact on the Next Generation:** Explore Bellew's influence on the next generation of boxers and aspiring

athletes. Discuss mentoring roles, motivational engagements, and the ways in which he actively contributed to the development of emerging talents in the sporting world.

7. **Legacy Beyond the Ring:** Beyond his achievements in boxing, delve into the lasting legacy Bellew aimed to leave. Discuss his philanthropic endeavors, community engagement, and contributions to causes that extended beyond the confines of the boxing ring.

8. **Family and Personal Values:** Shed light on Bellew's personal values, especially his dedication to family. Explore how his family played a role in shaping his character, providing support during challenging times, and influencing the principles that guided his career.

9. **Adaptability and Versatility:** Discuss Bellew's adaptability and versatility, not only as a boxer but also in his transitions to media roles and other ventures.

Explore how his ability to adapt contributed to a multifaceted career and a legacy that transcends a singular domain.

10. **The Echo of Tony Bellew:** Conclude the chapter by examining the enduring echoes of Tony Bellew in the world of boxing and beyond. Explore how his life lessons and legacy continue to resonate, inspiring individuals to pursue their passions, overcome challenges, and leave a meaningful impact on the world.

In capturing the life lessons and legacy of Tony Bellew, "Ringside Reverie" provides readers with profound insights into the mindset of a remarkable athlete, offering valuable takeaways that extend far beyond the confines of the boxing ring.

CHAPTER 30: The Final Bell

"The Final Bell" marks a poignant chapter in "Tony Bellew: Ringside Reverie," capturing the emotions, reflections, and sense of fulfillment as the renowned boxer looks back on a career marked by passion, perseverance, and the pursuit of greatness. Here's a glimpse of what this chapter might encompass:

1. **The Closing Moments:** Set the scene for the final moments in the boxing ring. Capture the atmosphere, the crowd's energy, and Bellew's mindset as he approached the fight that would ultimately lead to the closing chapter of his boxing career.

2. **Reflections on the Journey:** Allow Bellew to reflect on the incredible journey that brought him to this moment. From the early days of boxing to the highs and

lows of his career, explore the milestones, challenges, and significant moments that shaped him as a fighter.

3. **The Weight of Emotions:** Convey the intense emotions that accompany the final bell. Explore the mix of adrenaline, nostalgia, and the awareness that this marks the end of a significant chapter in Bellew's life.

4. **The Last Bout:** Provide a detailed account of Bellew's last bout. Chronicle the strategic considerations, the ebb and flow of the fight, and the emotional resonance of each round as he faces his opponent in the ring for the final time.

5. **Farewell to the Ring:** Describe the moment Bellew bids farewell to the boxing ring. Whether through words, gestures, or a symbolic gesture, convey the significance of this moment as he takes his final steps away from the spotlight.

6. **Expressions of Gratitude:** Allow Bellew to express gratitude to those who supported him throughout

his career. From trainers and teammates to family, friends, and fans, explore the heartfelt acknowledgments that characterize his farewell.

7. **The Impact on the Sport:** Discuss Bellew's thoughts on the impact he made on the sport of boxing. Explore how he envisions his legacy within the context of boxing history and the influence he hopes to have on future generations of fighters.

8. **Life Beyond Boxing:** Delve into Bellew's vision for life beyond the boxing ring. Discuss his aspirations, whether in media, business, or personal pursuits, conveying the sense of purpose and optimism that accompanies the transition to a new chapter.

9. **Retrospective Analysis:** Offer a retrospective analysis of Bellew's overall career. Explore the highs, the lows, the lessons learned, and the evolution of his skills and mindset throughout the years, providing a comprehensive overview of his contributions to the sport.

10. **The Echo of the Final Bell:** Conclude the chapter by examining the echoes of the final bell. Explore how this moment reverberates not only in Bellew's life but in the collective memory of the boxing world, leaving an indelible mark on the sport.

"The Final Bell" serves as a poignant and reflective conclusion to "Ringside Reverie," offering readers a deeply personal insight into the emotions and reflections of a boxer as he takes his final bow from the stage he dedicated his life to – the boxing ring.

CHAPTER 31: Tony Bellew: A Puncher's Path

"Tony Bellew: A Puncher's Path" delves into the intricacies of the renowned boxer's journey, exploring the multifaceted aspects of his career both inside and outside the ring. Here's an outline of what this book could encompass:

1. **Genesis of a Puncher:** Begin with Bellew's early years, uncovering the origins of his interest in boxing. Explore the influences, mentors, and formative experiences that set him on the path to becoming a formidable puncher.

2. **The Sweet Science Unveiled:** Provide an in-depth look at Bellew's approach to the sweet science. Explore his training routines, sparring techniques, and the

development of his signature punching style that became a defining feature of his boxing identity.

3. **Rising Through the Ranks:** Chronicle Bellew's rise through the professional ranks. Detail his notable fights, victories, and the strategic considerations that propelled him forward in the competitive world of boxing.

4. **The Art of the Knockout:** Highlight Bellew's prowess in delivering knockout punches. Explore the technical aspects of his powerful punches, showcasing specific bouts where his knockout abilities took center stage.

5. **Beyond the Gloves:** Delve into Bellew's life outside the ring. Explore his personal experiences, relationships, and the balance he struck between the demands of professional boxing and his life beyond the gloves.

Tony bellew

6. **Iconic Bouts:** Showcase Bellew's most iconic and memorable bouts. Whether victories or challenges, analyze the strategies, narratives, and emotional intensity that defined these pivotal moments in his career.

7. **Life in the Limelight:** Explore Bellew's experiences in the limelight. Discuss the pressures, expectations, and the intersection between his public persona and private life as he navigated the challenges of being in the public eye.

8. **Media Roles and Commentary:** Transition into Bellew's roles in the media. Explore how he seamlessly integrated into commentary and analysis, providing viewers with unique insights into the sport he dedicated his life to.

9. **Strategic Transitions:** Discuss Bellew's strategic transitions throughout his career. Whether moving up in weight classes, facing new opponents, or transitioning to roles outside of active competition, explore the strategic decisions that shaped his journey.

10. **Legacy of a Puncher:** Conclude the book by examining the lasting legacy of Tony Bellew as a puncher. Explore how his style, achievements, and impact on the sport continue to influence the boxing landscape and inspire future generations of fighters.

"A Puncher's Path" offers readers a comprehensive exploration of Tony Bellew's journey, focusing on his prowess as a puncher, the strategic choices that defined his career, and the multifaceted dimensions that make him a significant figure in the world of boxing.

Tony bellew

CHAPTER 32: Genesis of a Puncher

In the chapter "Genesis of a Puncher," readers are taken on a journey into the early life and formative experiences that ignited Tony Bellew's passion for boxing and set the foundation for his distinctive punching style. Here's an overview of what this chapter might encompass:

1. **Childhood Influences:** Explore Bellew's early years, painting a picture of his childhood environment. Discuss the influences, family dynamics, or local factors that contributed to his initial interest in boxing.

2. **Discovery of Boxing:** Detail the moment when Bellew first encountered the sport of boxing. Whether through a gym visit, a mentor, or a particular match that captured his attention, highlight the catalyst that sparked his interest in the sweet science.

3. **Inspiration and Idols:** Discuss the boxers or figures who inspired Bellew during his formative years.

Whether local heroes or international icons, explore how these role models influenced his perception of the sport and shaped his aspirations.

4. **Early Training Days:** Take readers into the early days of Bellew's training. Explore his initial experiences in the gym, the learning process, and the dedication he exhibited as he began to hone his skills in the art of boxing.

5. **Mentors and Coaches:** Introduce key mentors and coaches who played a pivotal role in Bellew's development as a puncher. Discuss the guidance, training philosophies, and lessons imparted by those who recognized and nurtured his potential.

6. **Amateur Career Beginnings:** Chronicle Bellew's entry into the amateur boxing scene. Explore his early competitions, victories, and the lessons learned from the amateur circuit that laid the groundwork for his transition to the professional ranks.

Tony bellew

7. **Defining Moments:** Highlight defining moments in Bellew's early boxing career. Whether a particular fight, a significant win, or a learning experience from a loss, delve into the pivotal events that shaped his identity as a puncher.

8. **Physical and Mental Development:** Discuss the simultaneous development of Bellew's physical prowess and mental resilience. Explore how he cultivated not only the physical attributes necessary for punching power but also the mindset required for success in the ring.

9. **Strategic Evolution:** Touch upon the strategic evolution of Bellew's punching style. Discuss how he adapted and refined his technique over time, incorporating lessons from both successes and challenges encountered during the early stages of his career.

10. **Early Indications of Punching Power:** Conclude the chapter by highlighting early indications of Bellew's

punching power. Whether through notable knockouts or displays of raw strength, convey the first glimpses of the formidable puncher he was destined to become.

"Genesis of a Puncher" immerses readers in the foundational experiences that molded Tony Bellew's passion for boxing and laid the groundwork for the powerful punching style that would define his remarkable career.

CHAPTER 33: Early Indications of Punching Power

The chapter on "Early Indications of Punching Power" delves into specific moments and bouts that showcased Tony Bellew's burgeoning strength and punching prowess during the early stages of his career. Here's an exploration of the key indications that marked him as a formidable puncher:

1. **Amateur Highlights:** Begin by revisiting notable moments in Bellew's amateur career that hinted at his punching power. Highlight specific bouts where he demonstrated a knack for delivering impactful punches, garnering attention and anticipation for his transition to the professional ranks.

2. **Debut in the Professional Arena:** Explore Bellew's debut as a professional boxer. Discuss the initial reactions from fans, opponents, and pundits regarding the power he showcased in his punches during those early professional fights.

3. **Signature Knockouts:** Highlight specific knockouts that became early signatures of Bellew's punching power. Whether through perfectly executed combinations, devastating body shots, or explosive finishes, delve into the moments that left an indelible mark on his opponents.

4. **Strategic Mastery:** Discuss how Bellew's punching power became intertwined with strategic mastery. Explore instances where he effectively set up opponents, capitalized on their vulnerabilities, and strategically deployed his power punches to secure victories.

5. **Dominance in Weight Classes:** Examine Bellew's performances as he climbed through different weight

classes. Discuss how his punching power translated
across these categories, showcasing his adaptability and
effectiveness as a puncher regardless of the division.

6. **Notable Opponents Impacted:** Explore the
reactions of notable opponents who experienced Bellew's
punching power firsthand. Whether through interviews,
post-fight comments, or analyses from fellow fighters,
capture the impact he left on those who faced him in the
ring.

7. **Audience and Fan Reactions:** Highlight the
reactions of audiences and fans to Bellew's early displays
of punching power. Dive into the excitement generated
by his explosive performances and the anticipation that
surrounded his fights as a rising star in the boxing world.

8. **Media Recognition:** Discuss how the media
recognized and celebrated Bellew's punching power.
Explore articles, commentaries, and analyses that
underscored the significance of his ability to deliver

impactful and memorable punches during this phase of his career.

9. **Training Regimen:** Offer insights into Bellew's training regimen and how it contributed to the development of his punching power. Discuss specific exercises, techniques, and approaches that played a role in enhancing his strength and effectiveness as a puncher.

10. **Early Achievements:** Conclude the chapter by summarizing Bellew's early achievements that were directly linked to his punching power. Whether title victories, notable rankings, or industry accolades, emphasize how his prowess as a puncher contributed to his early success.

"Early Indications of Punching Power" provides readers with a detailed exploration of the moments, opponents, and strategic elements that marked Tony Bellew as a rising force in the boxing world, showcasing his formidable punching abilities from the outset of his professional journey.

CHAPTER 34: The Art of Boxing

Tony Bellew: The Art of Boxing," the narrative weaves together the triumphs, challenges, and the enduring legacy of the renowned boxer. Here's an overview of what this book conclusion might encompass:

1. **The Final Bow:** Begin by capturing the atmosphere of Tony Bellew's retirement or final fight. Reflect on the emotions surrounding his last moments in the ring, the cheers of fans, and the acknowledgment of a career that left an indelible mark on the sport.

2. **Legacy in the Sweet Science:** Discuss Bellew's legacy within the context of the sweet science. Explore how his unique style, strategic prowess, and punching power contributed to a lasting impact on the sport of boxing, leaving an imprint for future generations.

3. **A Champion's Journey:** Take readers on a retrospective journey through Bellew's career highlights.

Tony bellew

Celebrate the victories, championship triumphs, and the instances where he overcame adversity, showcasing the breadth of his achievements as a true champion.

4. **Evolution Beyond the Ring:** Delve into Bellew's evolution beyond the boxing ring. Explore his transition to media roles, commentary, and other ventures, illustrating how his influence extended beyond the confines of active competition and into the broader world of sports and entertainment.

5. **Personal Growth and Reflection:** Reflect on Bellew's personal growth throughout his career. Discuss how the challenges he faced, both inside and outside the ring, contributed to his maturation as an athlete, a public figure, and a person navigating the complexities of life.

6. **Impact on the Next Generation:** Explore Bellew's impact on aspiring boxers and the next generation of athletes. Discuss his mentorship roles, motivational engagements, and how he actively contributed to the

development of emerging talents, passing on the knowledge gained from his own journey.

7. **A Puncher's Legacy:** Emphasize the lasting legacy of Tony Bellew as a puncher. Discuss the iconic knockouts, the strategic mastery, and the memorable moments that solidified his reputation as a force to be reckoned with in the art of delivering powerful, precise punches.

8. **Gratitude and Acknowledgments:** Allow Bellew to express gratitude to those who played a role in his journey. From trainers and teammates to family, friends, and fans, convey his appreciation for the support that accompanied him throughout his career.

9. **The Echo of Tony Bellew:** Conclude by examining the echoes of Tony Bellew in the boxing world. Explore how his legacy continues to resonate, inspiring individuals to embrace the art of boxing, persevere through challenges, and leave a meaningful impact on the sport.

10. **The Art Beyond Boxing:** Wrap up by highlighting how Tony Bellew's legacy extends beyond the technicalities of boxing. Discuss the artistry in his approach, the strategic nuances he brought to the sport, and the enduring beauty of his contributions to the sweet science.

In the final chapter of "The Art of Boxing," readers are left with a comprehensive and reflective portrait of Tony Bellew's journey, showcasing the artistry, the power, and the indomitable spirit that defined his remarkable career in the world of boxing.

Tony bellew

.

Printed in Great Britain
by Amazon

abbf038d-15f4-44d9-8edc-94881c024ae2R01